TEACHING CHRISTIANITY

A World Religions Approach

Foreword by Ninian Smart
Edited by Clive Erricker

L

LUTTERWORTH PRESS

Cambridge

The Lutterworth Press
PO Box 60
Cambridge
CB1 2NT

British Library Cataloguing in Publication Data:
A catalogue record is available from the British Library.

ISBN 0 7188 2634 5

First published 1987
Revised edition first published 1995

Printed in Great Britain by
The Ipswich Book Company

Contents

List of Illustrations

List of Contributors

Alan Brown Religious Education Schools Officer for the Church of England General Synod Board of Education; Director of the National Society Religious Education Centre, Kensington

Peter Curtis Senior Lecturer in Religious Studies, Trent Polytechnic, Nottingham

Peter Doble Director, the York Religious Education Centre

Clive Erricker Senior Lecturer in Religious and Professional Studies, King Alfred's College, Winchester

Cherry Gould Co-ordinator for Religious Education, Berkshire Education Authority

Mary Hayward Deputy Director, the York Religious Education Centre

Nora Horrigan Head of Religious Studies, Hardley Comprehensive School, Fawley, Hampshire

David Minton Co-ordinator of Personal Development, Benjamin Britten High School, Lowestoft, Suffolk

David Morling Head of Religious Education, Bishop Luffa Church of England Comprehensive School, Chichester, West Sussex

David Naylor Adviser for Religious Education, Hampshire Education Authority

John Rankin Director of the Chichester Project, formerly Head of Religious Studies, West Sussex Institute of Higher Education

Trevor Shannon Director of the Senior School, Forest School, London

Harry Stephens Senior Teacher and Head of Religious Studies, Westwood St Thomas's Church of England Upper School, Salisbury

Angela Wood Advisory teacher for Religious Education, Hounslow and Lecturer at West London Institute of Higher Education

Foreword

By Ninian Smart

Clive Erricker and his colleagues have here produced a clear and practical guide to the teaching of Christianity as a world religion. For me it is a sign of the fruition of many years work which some of us have been undertaking in the field of education. In the last quarter of a century there have been great advances in religious education. It has become recognised that we live in a global city in which there are people of many faiths, and that in Britain ours is a pluralistic society. It always was to some extent, but this fact was concealed by public rhetoric and by the existence of religious establishment. More recently, the activities of the Shap Working Party on World Religions, the foundation of religious studies in universities, the Lancaster projects on religious education, the work of John Hick and his colleagues in Birmingham, the attitudes of many enlightened educationalists such as HMIs and County Advisers — to mention only some of the forces at work — have combined with the dedication of forward-looking teachers to produce a somewhat different atmosphere.

I remember once when I accompanied some colleagues (Donald Horder and David Naylor among them) to Northern Ireland to stimulate interest in the new RE. We hoped that our new dedication to empathy, pluralism and openness might help the situation there. We put on a conference in Coleraine, to which came a number of Protestant and Catholic teachers including a few nuns. David Naylor put on a video-taped specimen lesson to children in a local school on Buddhism. The message was: if you can do this kind of thing with Buddhism why not also with Christianity? The nuns especially seemed enthusiastic. I always hoped that pioneering ways of teaching "other" religions would ultimately influence the teaching of Christianity. A few years ago I even very boldly wrote a book on Christianity, *The Phenomenon of Christianity* (1979), trying to look at it as one might look at any religion and trying to loosen up our vision of the faith. It is more exciting that way, I believe. I used the book in the University of California in 1980 for an introductory class. A student approached me at the end. He said that as a result of the course he had converted to the faith. I was taken aback: he remarked, however, that Christianity seen with warmth and impartiality, with a kind of understanding and open dispassion, was more appealing. More appealing though than what? I think he had in mind the frequently boring modes of presenting Christianity in a preachy way, or with the underlying assumptions of commitment.

The fact is that much of traditional teaching of Christianity has proceeded on false assumptions and has been quite unrealistic. It has been biblically based without any real attempt to see how the Bible has functioned in various Churches and in human experience. It has cut out great swathes of the tradition because of ideological attitudes. It has done very little to illuminate the range of Christian experience. If I teach a course on Buddhism, would I dream of leaving out meditation? Yet often Christianity is taught without any fieldwork and without reference to sacramental practice, Christian art, and so forth. Well, things are improving now, and though I believe that Christianity is by and large (especially in higher education) the worst taught of the great religions, we still can take heart from the effects of modern educational approaches on the curriculum.

And this book will with its range and practical detail be appealing I am sure to practitioners of the hard art of religious education. Clive Erricker and his colleagues have worked well in providing a useful tool for the classroom. Who knows? They might even make a few converts!

Some have criticised the phenomenological approach to world religions and the principles of dialogue. But what we need to do to be fair to our subject matter is to hold up a mirror to humans' various religious cultures. If what is seen in the mirror is beautiful then some who gaze in the mirror will fall in love. There is no deep divide between phenomenology and witness: but witness is self-defeating if it occurs in the classroom. Rightly, because we have no right to intrude our own commitments unequally upon students. We have to nurture knowledge and freedom. The world religions approach is committed to these aims. I wish this book every success.

Ninian Smart

University of Lancaster

University of California, Santa Barbara

Introduction

The aim of this book is to share some approaches to the teaching of Christianity as a world religion with practising teachers, students, lecturers in education and all those concerned with the quality of Religious Education and the Humanities in schools.

Approaches to Religious Education have changed a great deal over the last hundred years but never more so than since the 1944 Act. One of the most significant developments has been the serious introduction of the teaching of a number of major religious traditions in schools, usually embracing Judaism, Islam, Hinduism, Sikhism and Buddhism. Now it is also possible to follow examination options in these at 16+.

Underlying this new content has been a new approach. Broadly speaking this has emphasised the need to be initially non-judgemental in teaching about any religious tradition. Whatever one's own standpoint and beliefs, empathy and openness are the key terms. This has repercussions for the teaching of Christianity. It too is a world religion and as such demands the same approach as any other. But given that many Religious Education teachers are Christians, this becomes a very sensitive and subtle issue. We may acknowledge the need to teach about another's religion but teaching about one's own religion in the same way may be thought to involve further implications and make unacceptable or impossible demands. For many teachers of Religious Education this can be a real dilemma because it touches upon their own commitments and sensibilities. Teaching Christianity as a world religion becomes the biggest stumbling block of all, a test case for the whole 'world religions' approach.

This book takes up the issue of how this approach can be applied to teaching Christianity and tries to contribute to it through argument and example. It does so in three sections which follow on logically from each other and together attempt a comprehensive treatment from reflection on the challenges involved for education generally, and Religious Education in particular, to classroom examples of what this approach means in practice.

At the same time we do not wish to give the impression that all the answers are here. This collection of papers has a rather different aim. We hope most of the major questions that the 'world religions approach' raises are debated in the first section of the book, 'Approaches'. We hope the question of what is to be taught about Christianity and how this could be done is given some initial content in the second section, 'Aspects'. The third section, 'Practice', presents some examples of classroom teaching of diverse kinds and in different situations with regard to age group and the type of community within which each school is situated. In each case what is recorded in the article has been done in the classroom successfully. Doing things this way round has not been easy but we felt it was important that, rather than writing articles on what could be taught, we offer what has actually been done. Teaching methods and learning processes are highlighted in this way and the teacher writing each article was asked to be clear in presenting these as well as the content of the lessons. Methods vary greatly, reflecting, amongst other things, the differing personalities and preferred strategies of the teachers concerned. We believe this variety will add to the value of the whole. Also in this section are three articles reflecting on issues affecting good practice, namely school provision, assessment and the quality of resources available.

The whole collection across all three sections is offered as a stimulus to both teaching and debate. For teachers, discussion with colleagues often provides the greater impetus to effective teaching. We hope we have provided a structured and formalised example of this.

Thinking in curriculum terms, within Religious Education and other areas of Humanities such as World Studies, Social Studies and Political Education, there are many overlapping questions being debated which we hope we have contributed to effectively here.

The articles included express the viewpoints of their particular authors and *in this sense* the 'approach' of the book is not uniform. Each of the Chichester Project's other productions is ultimately the author's own work, endorsed as valuable, but not necessarily wholly agreed with, by individual Project members. The same is true for the articles in this collection. For this reason certain articles stand out as particularly provocative, notably David Minton's on the political dimension of Christianity and Clive Erricker's on Christianity in its cultural contexts. These articles address themselves to two ways in which the phenomenological description of Christianity has so far received less attention. If these articles give rise to constructive debate they will have performed their function.

This publication should not be regarded as a handbook to accompany the Chichester Project textbooks. It is entirely independent of them. Naturally it refers to them in passing and uses material from them in certain articles but the textbooks are not necessary in order to implement any of the suggestions made. Rather this collection is presented in the spirit and style of a symposium which we hope will prove to be inspiring and of practical value.

SECTION A

In this section there are five articles. *John Rankin's* opening article includes a history of the debate over how Religious Education should be taught and points to some of the presently unresolved questions and confusions that remain. He offers concisely argued principles on which to base a way forward.

Alan Brown explores the difficulties involved in approaching a world religion with respect to the categories through which it expresses itself. He then concentrates on how this applies to Christianity. Each religion has its own unique structure, and we should recognise structural differences to avoid simplistic comparison.

Peter Doble addresses the problem of openness and commitment in an imaginative manner. How can a teacher committed to a particular tradition teach in an open way? Whereas Alan Brown asks Christians to be open in their approach to other religions, Peter Doble asks that Christians be open in their approach to their own. He grounds this educationally by presenting 'dialogue' as 'one of the most precious of human skills'.

David Minton's article is a probing analysis of one aspect of Christianity: its political dimension. He investigates Christian responses to political situations within an historical framework emanating from the Old Testament and suggests what the implications of this are for the presentation of Christianity in the classroom and in the curriculum.

Clive Erricker examines the meaning of Christian pluralism by looking at the way Christianity expresses itself within different cultural contexts. This is not so much a study of 'denominations' but of the way in which Christians understand their beliefs in relation to other commitments, whether to their country, to a particular social order or cultural ideal.

SECTION B

In this section there are six articles. *Trevor Shannon* suggests how teaching about Jesus can include both an examination of the Jesus of History and an understanding of the Christ of Faith. He also offers concrete examples related to classroom teaching.

Peter Curtis speaks of presenting the Bible as the Christian's guide. Approaching it in this way helps us to reflect on our own aims in teaching about it and helps pupils understand its uses and value for Christians and what makes it special. He offers a typology of the literature it contains as a prerequisite for this.

John Rankin argues forcibly that worship is a way of approaching Christianity that avoids the difficulty of theological propositions by starting with practice. He emphasises that worship is also most often dynamic and communal, which highlights the concept of sharing and the notion of the Church, both of which are essential to a correct perception of Christianity.

Mary Hayward suggests that festivals impinge on the public consciousness more than any other aspect of Christianity and provide the most accessible route into it. However, she warns, festivals have many layers of meaning and understanding their significance rather than offering simple descriptions of them is what must be aimed at. Her model for exploring Christian festivals is an excellent example of this.

Alan Brown makes the statement that Christianity's concern with the fulfilment of the individual paradoxically can only be carried out if that person is identified as part of the Christian community — the Body of Christ. It is this that makes a study of Christian communities essential. He then examines the contrasts that follow: communities can be permanent and provisional, a unity and a collection of individuals, involve freedom and discipline, stability and growth. To understand Christian communities, we have to see what these contrasts mean in practice by looking at specific examples.

Clive Erricker's article argues that Christian ethics is not a study of a set of values without disagreement. He exemplifies this by contrasting Christian legalism, based on the Ten Commandments, with the situation ethics movement that cites love (*agape*) as the basis of Christian ethical decision-making. He also examines the factors involved in making a moral decision in the context of such practical social issues as contraception and poverty, which have been particular concerns of the Roman Catholic Church in this century.

SECTION C

This section comprises ten articles. It is different in its method from the two preceding ones because it presents work done rather than approaches and activities commended. The articles included do not represent a common approach to Christianity in any respect except the wish to do justice to it as a world religion, in the sense explained earlier in the Introduction. By design these articles reveal the difficulties this has involved as well as the achievements made.

Angela Wood's article is based on work done in a multicultural setting in London on different denominational expressions of Christianity. It reflects the different observations and concerns of pupils from diverse backgrounds and Angela's ability to take both them and the subject equally seriously.

Nora Horrigan explains how a particular teaching methodology can be used to explore the meaning of prayer in Christianity through looking at a day in the life of the Pope. The pupils' responses reveal how what may appear to be a distant subject in terms of their experience can be made both interesting and enriching.

David Minton's example of teaching about Christian ethics is drawn from differing teaching situations. He uses the notions of 'mottoes' and 'logos' to make some difficult ideas concrete and accessible. He also considers the critical question of what is specifically Christian about Christian ethics.

Clive Erricker approaches Christian experience and understanding Christian views of life through the use of visual material. He concentrates on three specific skills: avoiding caricature, understanding representation and making associations.

Cherry Gould talks about visiting Christian places of worship by thinking through how to prepare for, go about and follow up a visit. She also points out some of the things that should be focused upon, such as the variety of Christian places of worship but also the notion of their all belonging to one Christian family.

David Morling highlights the notions of trust and risk involved when teaching about Christian belief. He compares this with other modes of enquiry such as searching for scientific knowledge. For this he uses the work of Marie and Pierre Curie as an example.

Harry Stephens reflects on teaching about Jesus to a mixed-ability class of 13 year olds. Considering the person of Jesus as a puzzle, the pupils seek, by varying means, to understand the puzzle. He explains in particular detail how art can help bring this study to life.

In the final three articles, *David Naylor* advises on what provision a teacher needs in terms of time and resources, to carry out his teaching effectively.

Alan Brown discusses the role and methods of assessment that are appropriate to teaching Christianity.

Mary Hayward provides valuable insight into how far available resources take seriously the need to study Christianity in an enlivening manner with the accent on the learning process involved.

The principles and methods of the approach used by the Chichester Project were set out inside the front cover of each of the textbooks produced. A copy of this statement can be found in the Appendix at the back of this book

Introduction to the Second Edition

Since the 1988 Education Act debate concerning the teaching of Christianity in schools has been a focus of attention. The Act determines that teaching should be non-denominational and advocates that children's understanding of the Christian tradition is of particular importance. Such an educational climate emphasises the importance of the approach offered by this book. In its second edition the chapter on examination and assessment and the bibliography for the teaching of Christianity have been updated. We hope that this volume will be of great practical help to teachers and indicate ways in which Christianity can be taught effectively.

Acknowledgements and Permissions

The publisher and authors would like to thank the following for permission to reproduce copyright material:
William Collins Ltd: extract from *The Phenomenon of Christianity* by Ninian Smart. Jonathan Cape Ltd: extract from *To Have or To Be?* by Eric Fromm. Penguin Books Ltd: extract from *Inside the Company: CIA Diary* by James Agee. The Observer Foreign News Service: extract from *The Observer Colour Supplement,* 5 November 1984. The Bodley Head: extract from *The Pope in Britain* by Peter Jennings and Eamonn McCabe. Edward Arnold Ltd: extract from *Words for Worship* by C. Campling and M. Davis. P. C. Schumacher: *The Morality Story in Christian Ethics.* Oxford University Press: extract from *The Pilgrim's Progress* by John Bunyan *The Oxford Anthology of English Literature,* edited by F. Kermode and J. Hollander, Vol. III (*The Restoration and the Eighteenth Century*). The Bible Societies and Collins: extracts from Genesis 2 and 3, *The Good News Bible,* © *American Bible Society 1976. The Times Educational Supplement:* extracts from 'Selecting the Best' by David Wright. Westminster Music Ltd: *Prayer to a Labourer* by Victor Jara. The Art Institute of Chicago: *American Gothic* by Grant Wood. Mark Donaghue: *Christus Victor.* DACS: *The Persistence of Memory* by Salvador Dali. Cosmopress, Geneva/ADAGP, Paris: *The Crucifixion* by Graham Sutherland.

Every attempt has been made to trace the copyright on all works reproduced in the publication. If any copyright has been unwittingly transgressed, or a necessary gratitude gone unexpressed, the editor and publisher offer their sincere apologies and will rectify any such oversight in future editions.

SECTION A
APPROACHES

1 Christianity as a world religion: the educational implications

John Rankin

There are three main elements in the debate about the role of Christianity in Religious Education. (I am here confining the discussion to *Religious Education* and I am not embarking on the quite different topic of a Christian theology of education.)

The three main elements are firstly, the nature of the religion itself; secondly, the way in which the educational enterprise is conceived; and thirdly, the cultural context in which that education takes place. By that third element I am asserting that any theory on which it is intended to base practice must take account of the actual context.

Part of the context is historical. How have these elements been understood in the past? Let us consider this last element.

THE CULTURAL CONTEXT

1944 and onwards

The 1944 Education Act laid down that *religious* instruction should be given in all county schools. It did not specify that the instruction should be Christian and indeed there is clear evidence that the government of the day resisted any attempt to have the word Christian inserted or even to be drawn into *any* prescription of aims or content. (See Starkings, D. in Jackson, R. (ed.) *Approaches to World Religions*, pp.56—66.)

Agreed Syllabuses were to be prepared by local authorities by means of a statutory conference. The conference was to consist of four committees. One of these represented the Church of England and another other *'religious denominations'*.

Note again that the word 'religious' was preferred to 'Christian'. The other two committees were to represent the local authority and the teachers.

Agreed Syllabuses

Nevertheless the resultant Agreed Syllabuses made it quite clear that Christianity was to be on the agenda. Even in syllabuses almost twenty years on, this was the case.

'We speak of Religious Education, but we mean Christian Education... the aim of Christian Education in its full and proper sense, is quite simply to confront our children with Jesus Christ.' (Birmingham, Agreed Syllabus, 1962, p.6.)

Thus, it was not only that Christianity was to be the agenda — it was to be the presentation of the 'challenge' of Christianity.

In terms of content most syllabuses worked from detailed Bible study — sometimes proposing a quite exhaustive programme.

In the 1960s educationists like Goldman and Loukes proposed a new style. Goldman instigated the notion of the 'life-theme' and Loukes the idea of 'problem solving'. Both were concerned that Religious Education should become more relevant to the pupils, more related to their existential concerns. Nevertheless neither of these thinkers conceived of anything other than Christianity as the possible outcome. They did not assume that all the pupils would become Christian but they did assume that *some* would and that the rest would lie on a line of partial acceptance down to rejection. These methods were seen as the *best* way to bring Christianity to their pupils' service. The West Riding Syllabus *Suggestions for Religious Education* reflected the kind of thinking of the time. The exploration of moral or social issues was to be illuminated by reference to relevant passages in the New Testament. The point I am making is that although the 1960s seemed like an upheaval in Religious Education, the assumptions about the *Christian* orientation of Religious Education were not challenged.

As one who was engaged in RE at the time, I can testify that it is very difficult to allow one's thinking to 'break out' of the assumptions which underlie your subject. Many of us felt uneasy about the privileged status of Christianity in the school syllabus and sought to quieten our scruples by adopting what we felt was an 'open stance'. In this we were perhaps more inspired by the stirring taking place in Christian theology than by educational theory. But the openness was *towards* Christianity. Some of us also struggled to give some heed to religions other than Christianity.

It proved difficult because we lacked the knowledge, training, resources and encouragement.

The 1970s

The Shap Working Party on World Religions in Education was founded in 1969 and it marks the beginning of the growth in world religions teaching. I would not wish to claim too much for the Working Party. Historically, it is always a moot point whether a particular institution *reflects* changes or *causes* them. Certainly, many members of the Working Party set about producing some more interesting and reliable texts for schools on religions other than Christianity.

In spite of some unfavourable reactions, it is nowadays inconceivable that courses in world religions would be absent from the curriculum of students training to be Religious Education teachers. But we still have not solved the problem of how this development is to be assimilated into the general conception of Religious Education.

Interest was stimulated − and indeed in some locations *imposed* − by the arrival of immigrants (particularly from India, Pakistan and, later, Asians from East Africa). In my view, although changes were stimulated and hastened by the arrival of immigrants, their arrival only served to highlight a situation which was inherently illogical and perhaps educationally indefensible.

Today

Where Religious Education occurs (and one must register in passing that in many schools it has finally disappeared!) some kind of world religions teaching is usually included. Often, however, it happens in condescending or patronising ways. Sometimes there is the deliberate attempt to suggest that Christianity is the only adequate religion. Even if that approach is not expressly pursued, other religions are treated as not worthy of more than passing interest. And when it comes to consideration of moral issues, Christianity still provides the standard sources for serious consideration by the pupils.

It was the Schools' Council Secondary RE project based at Lancaster which popularised the use of the words 'implicit' and 'explicit'. 'Implicit' RE was concerned with the pupils' search for meaning and 'explicit' RE was concerned with the detailed phenomena of religion. Religious Education was to be a dialogue between the implicit and explicit, a dialogue between the quest for meaning and the 'meaning giving' phenomena of religion. In fact this has never quite worked out and there is still an uneasy relationship between the protagonists of each type. Of course, it is a matter of degree. Nevertheless teachers of Religious Education can usually be divided according to whether they see their prime task as being to lead their pupils to find their own religious interpretation of life, or whether they place greater emphasis on *understanding* the beliefs and practices of religion.

The problems

The adoption of the logicality of including the teaching of non-Christian religions throws up problems for the hitherto assumed aims in teaching Religious Education. It has always been a subject of bitter controversy. In the period leading up to the 1944 Act acrimonious debate was primarily between the Church of England and non-Conformist Churches. The latter felt that the proposed provision for RE was in danger of giving the Church of England monopoly in spite of the inclusion of the Cowper–Temple clause (religious instruction 'shall not include any catechism or formulary which is distinctive of any particular denomination'.) This clause also played its part in the exclusive use of the Bible as a teaching source.

Today the arguments still rage in some parts of the country about the teaching of non-Christian religions. Vociferous objection usually arises out of fear and many LEA county councillors and others seem to feel that the whole stability of the nation's way of life is threatened by the introduction of 'foreign' religions.

Certainly, if religious 'instruction', in terms of the 1944 Act, is seen as the vehicle for bringing up children as honest, loyal, hardworking citizens, it is difficult to see how this could be achieved in a 'religious' way without assuming some form of 'religious' norms (viz. Christian norms). However, perhaps what this dilemma highlights is that the legislators, while well-intentioned, were mistaken in believing that their aims could best be achieved in this way. All attempts to study the effects of teaching according to the *assumed* intentions of the Act show that it is singularly unsuccessful when judged by its own aims. Fortunately the terms of the Act are such that they permit more liberal interpretation than the assumed ones.

New directions

1. The advent of visible numbers of ethnic minorities whose religion is not Christian or whose culture does not have a structure deriving from Christianity has drawn our attention to the anomaly of assuming that our society was homogeneous, even in 1944. If we have the ambition to foster the growth of a liberal democracy we do not wish people to be educated in their separate faith groups. Indeed most of us would, I think, want to assert that it is very important that our children are educated *together*. From a different point of view we do not wish Religious Education to be a subject in school divided up into discrete 'faith groups'. Instruction in one's 'own' religion is a matter for each faith group to organise. This does not mean that Religious Education in school should be abandoned. What we need in school is the opportunity to learn about religion in its many manifestations with the explicit purpose of fostering mutual understanding and respect. But the purposes of education are not only social and the study of religion is an induction into worthwhile knowledge for its own sake. The absence of Religious Education in school would diminish the quality of the educational curriculum in general.

2. The Cowper–Temple clause was designed to prevent proselytizing into

any particular church or denomination. When proselytizing *of any kind* is abandoned as an unworthy aim in Religious Education the need for the clause disappears and the teacher is free to use as content precisely those things which *are* distinctive of particular denominations. It is the 'distinctive' things which give a religion its shape, its specific concreteness and its link with the lives of people. When this is applied to Christianity we find that even within that inclusive title there is a need to understand the *variety* of practice and belief. Indeed it causes one to wonder what kind of 'all purpose' Christianity it was assumed children should be led to; a Christianity with no creed or formulary distinctive of any denomination looks rather bland and emaciated. Is it not better that children should understand the meaning and purpose of the church buildings scattered over the land, the meaning of the rites and ceremonies, and the reasons for specific beliefs devoutly held?

3.   The assumption that Christianity is the only locus of moral education should be discouraged. In our life together we should be looking for consensus — Christians, humanists, Muslims, Jews and all others as well. We cannot use the Bible as *the* consensus in a society as complex and multicultural as ours.[1] We can, however, at certain points consider the ethical demands of specific religions. To this extent Religious Education becomes an important place for the exploration and discussion of ethical issues.

PRINCIPLES

1 .   The nature of Christianity as a world religion is discussed elsewhere in this volume. One aspect of its nature is the assumption of truth. This is not of course unique to Christianity, but since the majority of RE teachers are drawn from a Christian background, it follows that Christian phenomena tend to be presented with greater conviction than the phenomena of other faiths.

Perhaps teachers need to learn the capacity of 'taking seriously' — taking seriously the offering of flowers to the Buddha, the pilgrimage to Mecca and bathing in the sacred Ganges, as well as the Eucharist. 'Taking seriously' is something less than 'practising' or 'advocating' but it is the style (perhaps the only style) which is educationally viable. There is decidedly little gain if Christian prayer is commended and Muslim prostration treated with a faint note of derision.

The same principle applies to the examination of the varieties of *Christian* expression. Christian history is punctuated by acts of extreme intolerance committed by one group or another, but the teacher has to 'take seriously' the positions adopted by all of them. Doubtless the teacher will have a view, and the pupils may well know what that view is. No teacher is exempt from the influence he or she has by virtue of their contact with young people and pupils would expect the teacher to have an opinion. Yet that can be a positive virtue provided teachers ensure that other views are 'taken seriously'.

2 .   There is little doubt that Christianity will provide the major part of the syllabus content in RE in Britain. Religious Education should provide some understanding and awareness of the culture in which pupils are living.

Equally they ought to learn how that culture is greatly affected by the contribution of other faiths.

I am aware that there are serious problems for some Christians in the idea that Christianity is presented as being 'one among others'. Yet as educationists we cannot easily accept a situation where the religion of one group of citizens is to be presented as superior to another.

APPROACHES

For reasons which we have seen, Christianity in the past has been taught overwhelmingly by means of the study of the Bible.

The Bible is the foundation document of Christianity but in itself it does not do justice to the study of Christianity. It is as if we expect pupils to 'begin again' and project the nature of Christianity from the foundation documents. But Christianity is a living faith and it has a history. Teaching about Christianity ought to begin with what Christians do, with what they feel to be important. That will, of course, include the Bible, but it is just as important to understand why the Bible is held in such esteem as it is to be introduced to form-criticism of the Gospels — perhaps more important! Christians also worship, build churches, keep festivals, have ethical principles, have conceptions of how we should live together and hold certain beliefs. The concrete, observable things that Christians do and say provide the best starting points.

Teaching about Christianity can also be incorporated in thematic teaching across religions, such as in a topic on 'sacred buildings', for example. The danger of 'across-religions' thematic teaching is that the status of a particular activity in one religion tends to be 'read into' another religion. In the example quoted, ideas about the church building can be 'read into' the synagogue or mosque or mandir. Of course they all share certain characteristics but their status and function vary significantly in each religion. However, thematic teaching is a useful way of improving awareness and for many pupils it has a more intrinsic motivation.

Nevertheless, for older pupils it is best not to encourage comparisons which are often superficial and misleading.

IS IT POSSIBLE?

There are those who would argue that it is impossible to teach any religion to which the teacher is not committed. The argument is that 'commitment' is not just something to be added on at the end of some other kind of religious knowledge, but is organically and essentially part of that knowledge. And if that is the case, it follows that only someone who is himself committed can convey this essence.

Unfortunately, if this argument is true then the whole enterprise of Religious Education in schools would have to be abandoned. We cannot have a situation where a subject can only be understood by means of some kind of life-commitment to it. At least we cannot have it in *school* because it would contradict the open, critical spirit of education. There are those who have come to precisely this conclusion. They argue that religion should not be taught in school: not because it is unimportant but because it is *too* important and that teaching 'without commitment' does violence to the essential nature of religion.

They are entitled to their view, of course, but that policy would still leave each faith community confined within its own prescriptions peering uncomprehendingly at the others. Furthermore, it is a sound educational principle that all human phenomena should be open for study and it would be a retrograde step to decide that certain areas of human behaviour were beyond comprehension unless you 'belonged'. I concede that, as in many human activities, there may be inner sancta understood only by the adepts and devotees. I concede that 'total' comprehension may be unattainable. However, I believe, together with many great thinkers, that nothing human should be beyond my grasp. If we say that mankind must live in groupings which are all mutually incomprehensible then it is a counsel of despair for the future.

The true difficulty is not so much in the degree to which each faith is idiosyncratic but in *how* to penetrate its significance, how to go beyond the surface forms to some understanding of the range of subjective perceptions of its adherents. This is another topic, and it has by no means been fully explored. It would be better if energy were directed in this direction rather than in exhaustive arguments about content.

We may not have arrived yet. But we need the conviction that it *is* possible.

CONCLUSION

The stance being advocated here, does not reduce the study of Christianity to one of description only. We are *not* faced, as so many pretend, with a polarised choice between 'teaching for commitment' and 'mere description'. There is a more realistic educational position of 'teaching for understanding' which involves description, certainly (and as an aside − we should not despise description and information; pupils are frequently hampered by ignorance of facts!), *but* involves also the excitement of the imagination, the genuine effort to understand what it *feels* like, what it *means* to a believer. Imagination is the device we use as human beings to come to an understanding of many things.

All that I have said so far, can be said from the point of view of an educationist of any faith, or of none.

But I wish to add that it can also be cogently argued from a position within the Christian faith. I cannot pursue the matter at length, but briefly it is this. Over the centuries Christianity has presented a fairly aggressive face to the world. Built into many traditional hymns are analogies of warfare and conquest. The world was to be saved by converting everyone to Christ.

I think that experience has taught many Christians that perhaps the very arrogance of that approach is mistaken; that it does not go well with the vision of the servant which Christians have in Christ; that they have perhaps mistaken the 'form' of the Church for the essence. They have come to acknowledge that God can speak to them through others; that 'loving one's neighbour' must at least mean *listening* to him; and that listening means being open to what he has to say. Being a Christian means believing in God's loving purposes and valuing others for what they are.

Of course it puts the faith as they understand it at risk, but perhaps they are being called to a greater faith. Christians are not being invited to 'deny' or 'diminish' their faith, but rather to demonstrate a greater faith, a greater generosity, a greater humility.

NOTES

1.   This does not mean that the Christian ethical tradition built into our institutions is diminished. On the contrary it is free to be valued more strongly for its own sake and it also allows for some *development* of an ethical base for our society which it badly needs.

2   Christianity and other religions

Alan Brown

'CHRISTIANITY' AND 'RELIGION'

To reach any understanding of this relationship one has to wrestle with quite difficult words like 'Christianity' and 'religion'. It is not enough to argue that the global term 'Christianity' is sufficiently monolithic to give a clear indication of what Christians feel or think about non-Christian religions. Indeed, it is not easy to define what we mean by 'religion' and there is little unanimity as to what constitutes a religion. By the same token it is not straightforward to define where one can draw the boundaries of Christianity. However, given this important caveat we can proceed without attempting to resolve it because we will, generally, be dealing with 'mainstream' religious traditions.

The point to be taken from the above is that of diversity, and of diversity within diversity. It is not adequate to say that, for example, 'all Lutherans believe there is no truth in any religion except Christianity', for while some Lutherans may agree with the statement, others will not. Equally the Roman Catholic Church could make conciliatory statements about people from non-Christian religions at Vatican II but that would not commit all Roman Catholics to that view. What it does do, however, is to give some indication of what Roman Catholic policy is on this issue. Various churches may have clear 'official' policies towards people of other religions, though individuals may feel more comfortable with their own view. It is often possible, however, to indicate a general line of thinking but difficult to make categorical statements.

This article looks at some of the problems involved when teachers look at the relationship between Christianity and other religions. It takes a number of issues − antagonism, paternalism, the structure of religion, truth and paradox − in order to draw attention to the dangers of generalisation and over-simplification.

ANTAGONISM AND PATERNALISM

Antagonism and paternalism polarise two very strong views held by some Christians. Antagonism need not degenerate into physical violence but the evidence of history suggests that at times religion (or Christianity in particular) has played a major role in inflammatory conflict. It is often more clearly demonstrated in the inability of a person of one religion to listen with sensitivity and understanding to a person from another religion. The other view is the paternalism found among certain Christians. Of course, this is no less antagonistic because it is also based upon insensitivity and lack of recognition of the other people's commitment. It is not easy to demonstrate this relationship but Christian attitudes to Judaism and Islam help to define the issue more closely, though it must be noted that what follows is a very general argument.

Christians, by the very foundation of their faith, see their roots firmly in Judaism, or perhaps more precisely, in the Jewish Scriptures. They argue that Jesus was the fulfilment of the scriptures (the Jewish Scriptures) and therefore while those have a use and a validity of their own they cannot retain the same primacy as they once had. This is an interesting argument, though not totally persuasive; for Christians who meet with Jews in dialogue soon notice that the Jewish Scriptures are used very differently from the Christian Old Testament to the extent that while the content is the same they appear almost to be different books.

The implication in this for 'confident' Christians is that the Jews have partially, but not completely, understood the scriptures, resulting in a patronising attitude, like that of a parent to a child who has not yet come to full understanding.

Islam claims that the Qur'an records the ultimate revelation of God and that it therefore supersedes the revelations that have been 'imperfectly recorded and understood' by Jews and Christians. This presents Christians with an interesting dilemma for while they might claim that the Jews have not fully understood, they too stand accused of failure to perceive. This interaction between these three religions provides an obvious case in which antagonism can play a part and the religious persecutions that have taken place as a consequence provide an unfortunate example in which Christians have been fully implicated.

In many respects Judaism, Christianity and Islam use similar models in order to express the profundity of their faith yet the apparent similarity is dangerous for it can result in false understanding. It appears, for example, that the term 'Messiah' would provide a convenient bridge between Judaism and Christianity but even an initial scratching of the surface shows that the two religions have come to interpret the word quite differently. This can be paralleled in other examples and is a salutary lesson to the teacher to take care when moving from one religion to another or teaching thematically.

One further example may illustrate the antagonism that can be inspired by a failure to respect the depth of feeling of another's faith. One may look at examples in the classroom such as the failure to respect the Qur'an — in the way the book is handled, the necessary ablutions, the careful placing of it after use, and the way the Muslim must always be mindful of its presence. This is a concept foreign to most Christians who use their Bible differently and perhaps do not handle their book in the same way. Similarly, the Torah Scroll has a specific place in Judaism and, although the teacher may make blanket statements about scriptures for convenience, the nuances, expectations and axioms in each religion are fundamentally different.

THE STRUCTURE OF RELIGION

Taking up the point mentioned above one has to realise that each religion has its own unique structure and that even within itself each religion may have different and distinct structures leading to different sorts of organisations. One of the values of RE is to try to help the pupil recognise the structural differences in religion so that simplistic comparisons may be avoided. Try to avoid making any comparison between other people's religion and your own (or the religion with which you are most familiar) — but take care, it is a demanding exercise.

How many syllabuses and textbooks take a 'Christian' model by looking at a 'founder', building, scriptures, worship, etc. without really thinking out whether such a structure is acceptable to other religions? This is not a deliberate attempt to distort a non-Christian religion but one suspects that some members of religions other than Christianity must mutter, 'If I was going there, I wouldn't leave from here.'

All humans search consciously and unconsciously for some means of classification, categorisation or construction, and religion may be too conveniently slotted into a category. As the majority of people in Britain are familiar with at least some aspect of Christianity, that religion is taken as the 'norm' through which all others will be studied. Obviously this has to have an effect on the teaching of religion. In spite of what is often said and written, it is comparatively rare to meet a secondary school pupil who knows nothing about Christianity. Most would recognise a church or be able to say something about Christmas, and the name 'Jesus' would strike a chord, although possibly not much more. This is not the case with other religions in this country. There is still little familiarity with, for example, Purim, Baisakhi, Eid-ul-Adha or what goes on inside a gurdwara. If pupils bring their own experience with them it is impossible for the teacher to ignore it and these experiences can be negative. One class of primary school children knew little about Judaism but were certainly aware of anti-semitic stereotypes. The teacher must break down familiar structures or stereotypes. Rather than say they are incorrect, he or she should help the pupil work through the more obvious examples of stereotyping in order to modify and refine them in the light of broader experience.

A QUESTION OF TRUTH

Where does truth lie? Which religion is correct? Are there not direct claims in the Christian scriptures which say that salvation is impossible unless one believes Jesus is the Son of God? Some religions do not claim to be the sole purveyor of ultimate truth; others, like Christianity, do claim to be the only *true* religion. How must this affect relations between religions? How does the teacher respond to questions about these absolute claims?

It would be convenient if there were one easy or straightforward answer — but there isn't. Some Christians do argue for the sole truth of their religion — some even argue that truth exists only in their particular type of Christianity. Still others argue that while truth lies quintessentially within the Christian religion, people of other religions have received a partial revelation and may be judged sympathetically. Again, other Christians would argue that Christianity represents only one of a number of religions all seeking the truth; each religion is different and one accepts whichever appears to be the most relevant. It is too simple, and, in fact, a distortion, to represent Christianity as having a straightforward view even though pupils are known to prefer black and white to shades of grey!

One way through this minefield is to consider a key concept in Christianity, for example, belief. The Christian religion, generally, places great emphasis on belief. There are a number of creeds, the best known being the Nicene Creed and the Apostles' Creed. Many years were spent honing and defining these areas of belief. Not all other religions place as much emphasis on belief as Christianity. Judaism places a special emphasis on practice — it has no creed. Islam has no creed in the Christian sense of the word though what is called the creed is in essence the fundamental affirmation of faith (There is no God but God and Muhammad is his prophet). Hinduism allows a wide variety of belief and practice. The threefold pronouncement of Theravada Buddhism cannot be called a creed in the Christian sense of the word:

I take refuge in the Buddha
I take refuge in the Dhamma
I take refuge in the Sangha.

Thus all the religions make different types of claim. They make different kinds of assertions of faith based upon belief, practice, experience, etc. so that it is inappropriate to juxtapose them unless a deep study is to be made. Pupils have to be encouraged to ask the correct questions, i.e. those questions that will carry them farther along the path of investigation. (This is not only relevant to RE, it is an educational objective appropriate to all subjects.) The teacher might help the pupil explore the question of truth by diverting questions away from the desire to know which religion is correct towards a more specific exploration of what each religion says and how each religion expresses itself. Truth questions are often more pertinent for the followers of a particular religion than they are for the student of religion.

A PARADOX

Paradox is no stranger to religion: it weaves in and out, baffling and extending the mind, trying to extend the finite into the infinite or bring the infinite within the grasp of the finite. Christianity has its own paradox in the person of Jesus — who is human yet divine in such a way that neither is diminished. To teach about Jesus, arguably the central focus of Christianity, is to teach about a paradox, for if one is to locate that which is distinctive about Christianity it lies in the beliefs and claims made by Christians for Jesus. Consequently, how the teacher relates the person of Jesus to other great religious leaders or prophets is crucial to the way in which Christianity approaches other religions. No other religion makes such a claim as the central feature of its faith. Thus the teaching about Jesus must be different from how the teacher approaches Guru Narak, Muhammad, Moses, etc. The distinction lies not only in the claims made about Jesus, it resides also in the position of Jesus within Christianity itself. Christians make 'impossible claims' for Jesus (or many of them do) that stretch beyond the claims made on behalf of others. This is not to deny the importance of the claims of other religions – it is to urge that the teacher looks for the central paradox, the 'impossible claim' of other religions in order to treat them with respect and integrity. One may, for example, speculate that the Qur'an is the 'impossible claim' of Islam, the Torah that of the Jews (or perhaps the theory of Election?). Where would such a claim be located for the Buddhist, the Hindu or the Sikh?

CONCLUSION

This article has been concerned to show how Christianity struggles in its relations with people of other religions. It struggles because it has no unanimous view. It does have apparent similarities but these mask grave divergences and subtle nuances. Its distinctiveness lies in the claims made for the person of Jesus yet because it has this distinctive focus, its structures, organisations, beliefs and practices must be different from those of other religions. The range of human ingenuity may limit variations of response but the philosophical and/or theological axioms mean that each religion is fundamentally different from another.

The issue for the teacher is not simply one of content – What shall I select from this or that religion? It is one of method – How shall I approach the teaching of this religion as opposed to the teaching of that religion in a way which most of its adherents would appreciate? Oddly enough, if the teacher can take these questions to heart then RE will transcend being simply informative because the pupil will join the teacher in solving the problems of inter-faith dialogue.

3 Commitment and an open approach to teaching Christianity

Peter Doble

Teaching Christianity in an open way raises problems about commitment. Some complain that British teachers are likely to be too committed to the Christian faith to be truly open; others complain that an open approach neuters Religious Education by taking all sense of commitment out of it. Additionally, some teachers will experience tension within themselves between their personal commitments as Christians and their professional commitments as teachers. It is necessary to be aware of these issues in order to consider the major question, namely, how may one teach the Christian tradition so that the believer's commitment emerges clearly as a central element in what is studied without the teacher's personal commitment getting in the way?

In an article of this length we can do no more than indicate some of the factors which need attention. The first section explores the concepts of openness and commitment; the second indicates something of the complexity of commitments in tension or conflict; while the third marks out some key causes for concern in the teaching of Christianity in Britain.

OPENNESS AND COMMITMENT

An open approach to Religious Education aims to bring about *understanding* of what it means to a believer to hold a religious view of life, and to do this a teacher generally adopts a 'third-party' perspective on what is being studied. That is, the teacher does not assume a pupil's prior commitment to or participation in the faith being studied, but rather looks with him from the outside in.

An open approach thus respects a child's autonomy, neither laying on him assumptions which his own experience cannot bear nor hoping to bring about his conversion to a specific faith or to a version of it. An open approach takes religious faith very seriously indeed because its intention is to bring about understanding. Its content is not simply limited to 'scripture' or 'divinity' but draws on mankind's religious experience so that a pupil may have an imaginative grasp of what it must be like to be a believer.

Of course, this approach raises many questions among which we shall attend solely to the relation of commitment to the open teaching of Christianity. Commitment generally indicates a long-term, self-imposed obligation to pursue a chosen rational goal or activity. Anything less than 'long-term' would take the notion in the direction of whim or fad. Anything less than 'self-imposed' or willingly embraced, would suggest that what was proposed was not the will of the whole person. Anything less than 'rational' might be said to have the character of obsession or eccentricity, or even sickness.

Commitment may be to people or to ideals. Long-term stability in personal relationships is commonly praised; a self, organised to be concerned for another, is usually accounted a healthier, more fulfilled person than the self anxious for its own ends. Commitment to an ideal or cause illustrates another feature of the concept: choice. Of the *many* possible ideals or values, a committed person has chosen *one* because it seemed proper to him, after reflection, to do so. Consequently, he is liberal rather than Tory or socialist, vegetarian rather than meat-eating, and so on. In any case, the choice brings about a long-term, self-imposed obligation to behave consistently. All humans are complexes of commitments; without them our lives are less than human.

Religious commitment is one example among many of our commitment-making, but, in the nature of the case, it is elevated above the others because it has the quality of *ultimacy*. It is from this commitment that other commitments flow; they are contingent upon it. Of course, since everyone, whether a religious believer or not, uses a limited number of axioms in understanding his own existence, and since these consequently have a measure of ultimacy, everyone has ultimate commitments however they may be formulated. Commitment presents problems to all teachers, not solely to religious believers.

Juxtaposition of the terms 'open approach' and 'commitment' has sparked off a debate that is still in its early stages, but this is the point at which to isolate some of its elements and to show them in interaction.

COMMITMENTS IN TENSION

Since we all have commitments which vary in intensity and scope it is not surprising that commitments are often in conflict and, much more frequently, in tension, certainly among people, less obviously within an individual person. Yet, for example, a pacifist may also be committed to respecting and defending the personal rights of other people: moral problems are essentially commitments in conflict.

Discussion of commitment in Religious Education needs to be set in this much larger context or its proper proportions will be lost. On the other hand, the issues must be reduced to a size which can be handled comfortably, so some very important factors are omitted from the following discussion.

Imagine entering a classroom to watch an RE lesson; some key commitments are in tension.

The teacher

Consider the teacher, John. He has not divested himself of all commitments before coming through the door; people are not like that. One, probably the most profound of all his commitments, may be John's religious commitment. He believes talk about God to be meaningful; he is both convinced that God *is* and that this conviction is well-founded because it is verified by his experience. His picture of God has been formed by an interaction between the tradition in which he stands and his own experience so far. This picture lays claims on him; if that is what the most real is like then he, John, ought to be...and a whole train of moral, social and political obligations come in the rear of this 'great commitment' to God. For example, he belongs to a specific community with its own emphasis: it is not enough to call him Christian for John is a Baptist, evangelical, tending to emphasise the authority of the Bible, with a 'low' view of liturgy and a strong emphasis on his local Christian church as the family of God. The variations possible in such a construct can tend to infinity because teachers, like everyone else, are unique people.

John also brings professional commitments into the classroom, commitments which began when during his professional education he learned to put the child at the centre of his concern. He learned that education is quintessentially the helping of pupils to move towards personal maturity, that is, towards becoming the most complete, stable, self-fulfilled persons possible for them. Of course each staff room has its cynic and its world-weary doubter, but, by and large, the teaching profession, of whom John is typical, remains distinguished by its profound commitment to nurturing the growth of the child in body, mind and spirit.

Then, John brings with him his commitment to his subject. He *chose* Religious Studies and then Religious Education; its mastery cost him much effort; his skills and knowledge in this discipline contribute to his self-identity. Because the subject matters to him John is committed to helping others share its interest, value and worth.

Furthermore, his school subject, Religious Education, is defined by an Agreed Syllabus. By continuing in employment John has accepted a contractual commitment to teach his subject within the framework of intentions, approaches and attitudes which constitute that syllabus and represent a consensus.

The students

John's pupils also have commitments. This is not the place to explore the provisional or emergent nature of commitment in a child moving towards maturity; suffice to note that socio-familial solidarity, preliminary but firmly-held *personal* commitments (and others half-formed and still fragile) may characterise the child. At any stage in his young life the pupil's world is created by his commitments: they make for his security and are a precondition of his growth. Some will be shed if he is to be himself, and new ones made that are especially *his* and not 'just' those handed down to him. Both the vulnerability and expectation of the child must figure large in John's accounting of his responsibility: how does one take RE seriously without threatening or limiting the pupil? The sheer variety of experience which children bring to RE in a plural and multicultural society is daunting and must exercise a considerable influence on the planning of work.

Other aspects

Religious Education, probably more than any other area of the curriculum, is subject to outside agents — parents, governors and the LEA probably figuring most largely. For each group of agents a variety of commitments may be suggested, but only a few can be noted here. Parents may well have a clear expectation of what a school ought to do for their children; they may also have expectations of what should — or should not — happen in an RE lesson, their religious and ideological commitments having an intimate relation with the way they want their children to grow up.

Similarly, governors and the LEA have commitments relating to their responsibility to provide education for pupils. A kind of contract exists between the LEA and the electorate, between the governors and the parents of school children, a commitment formed by democratic consensus.

These complexes of commitments are a minefield for every RE teacher. Parents and governors properly ask whether John can be *trusted* to deal with the sensitive issues of religious commitment in ways that are consonant with what they understand by education. One teacher may be suspected of being a pseudo-educator, a slightly disguised missionary; another may face, on the one hand, his own internal questioning about the propriety of what he is doing, and, on the other hand, the charge that by 'neutrality' or 'objectivity' he has robbed religious faith of what makes it what it is — the passion of commitment. What can be said of these charges?

COMMITMENT AND THE CLASSROOM

At this point, after exploring the notions of commitment and openness, we can return to the major issue with which we began: how may one so teach the Christian tradition that the believer's commitment emerges clearly as a central element in what is studied without the teacher's personal commitment getting in the way? This question may be approached along four routes.

Teacher commitment and Christian diversity

Personal religious commitment can, but need not, distort a presentation of Christianity. How can this be?

Because there is no such entity, the concept 'Christianity' is an abstraction from the real world in which Christian tradition expresses itself in a variety of responses to Jesus's story and to the ever-growing tradition which flows from it. Consequently, John belongs to a specific Christian community; this has its own sense of history, its own tradition, distinctive worship, interpretation of scripture and its own doctrinal emphasis. Christians from other traditions may be as alien to John as adherents of other religions. He holds his commitment among a bewildering variety of positions – Catholic/Protestant, church/chapel, fundamentalist/liberal, fringe/mainstream – each of which contributes to the concept 'Christianity'.

How is he to ensure that his own commitment does not so select and guide the presentation of material that what children learn is simply that form of Christianity to which John is committed?

One solution is to work with a model of Christianity which is deliberately larger than the dimensions of his own commitment, embracing the unities and disunities of what is properly a group of religions centred on Jesus. It is worth his taking pains over this model for it is not only his defence against partisanship but one determinant of how interesting and authentic John's presentation of Christianity will be. While this is not the place to explore the possibilities and frustrations of model-making it will be useful to sketch one that John might find helpful. In this model Christianity is:

A FAMILY OF TRADITIONS   – Orthodox Catholic,
                            Protestant, non-white,
                            indigenous and fringe;

COMMUNITIES IN PROCESS   – developing liturgies,
                            interpreting scripture,
                            encountering new cultures,
                            growing through mission;

A CLUSTER OF FAITH   – doctrinal formulations
SYSTEMS   interacting with
                            ever-changing world views
                            and reinterpreting their
                            primal vision;

FAITH ENCOUNTERING THE   – Christian moral and
WORLD   political responses to the
                            primal vision, diverse,
                            sometimes contradictory, yet
                            with degrees of unity.

Within such a model John's own religious commitment will have an appropriate proportion: his vision of and commitment to Christianity, with all that that implies, will be inescapable.

A teacher's religious and professional commitments

If a teacher has a professional commitment to work with a model of Christianity larger than that which carries his own religious commitment and at the same time to ensure that the distinctiveness and ultimacy of Christian commitment is a part of his pupils' understanding of Christianity, how is he to relate this to his personal religious commitment? It is at this point that some teachers experience their greatest difficulty, for is not one's religious commitment the ultimate, overriding, self-imposed obligation, and should not one's professional obligations be subordinate to it? Presumably, the answer is 'yes', otherwise religious commitment would not have the ultimacy which defines it. Consequently, any proposal to teach Christianity in an open way appears at first sight to diminish the significance of a teacher's Christian commitment — but only at first sight.

Consider the possibility that an open approach may be entailed by a certain sort of Christian commitment. Perhaps one might construct a continuum on which teachers may locate their personal situation. At one end of this continuum would be those who recognise and work with the fact that there are many styles of being Christian while at the other end are those who identify being Christian with that version they have embraced. Pluralists recognise that Christian belief has worked with many differing pictures of God, each of which entails its own styles of daily living, among which will be an educational style. So there is not necessarily a conflict between religious and professional commitment, rather a probability that some forms of Christian commitment will lead to an open approach. Among those professionals who have hammered out an open approach to RE, and to Christianity in particular, many have a serious Christian commitment.

Serious problems present themselves to teachers at the other end of the spectrum, that is, to those whose commitment allows no picture of God other than the one they personally hold and whose single-minded aim is to replicate their style of being Christian in all whom they meet. Teachers from this group have a powerful urge to evangelise and do not seriously consider any other form of teaching. Their problem is simple: how can they properly serve the county schools of a pluralist Britain whose educational aims differ significantly from those of the teacher's own group? While integrity demands that they find a subject other than RE to teach, realism recognises that such teachers develop different responses: some continue to teach as they have always taught; others swallow their scruples and try the form and content of open teaching, though their heart is not in it and their conscience is bruised.

Commitment in Christian diversity

One of the most vigorous complaints about an open approach to the teaching of Christianity has been that it robs faith of its passion by reducing the study of religion to the study of phenomena in some objective way. Not so. To understand what it means to hold a Christian view of life is to understand that if God *is*, and that if He is the God and Father of the Lord Jesus Christ, then ethical, social and political consequences follow. Furthermore, because the prior commitment to God has an ultimacy which raises it above other commitments, because it is central to the believer's life, holding its parts together in a meaningful unity, the whole complex of commitment and consequence is suffused with emotion, even passion – these things *matter*.

The variety of Christian traditions in Britain makes this clear. During the seventeenth century various religious parties passionately believed their own expression of Christian faith to be the true one. Some believed that the Roman Catholic Church alone handed on apostolic truth and the hope of salvation. Others were certain that the Church of England, the Catholic Church reformed of its accretions and political pretensions, was what God intended for this realm. Within that Church a struggle was taking place for its soul: some wanted to follow John Calvin in banishing the remnants of Catholicism, and thereby bring about a root and branch purifying of the Church, while others could accept neither Calvin's depiction of God's dealing with people nor his apparent unconcern for centuries of Christian tradition. Yet others wanted a far more radical dissociation of believers from tradition, creed, hierarchy and liturgy. Their conflicting commitments had powerful results including martyrs and much suffering. It is in the nature of such 'basic' commitments, whether religious or not, that they are intimately associated with emotion and no one is religiously literate until he has grasped this fact.

But such commitment is also the mainspring of the good: social reformers, saintly people and ordinary folk who struggle at great cost, wherever they are, for love and justice demonstrate the results of commitment to live as though God is Love.

Classroom teaching that fails to include 'commitment' among its phenomena has simply failed to portray Christianity. Open teaching is not passionless.

Teacher commitment as a resource for Religious Education

Talk of a teacher's commitment 'getting in the way' of an open approach is positively misleading. It suggests that religious commitment is somehow professionally disreputable and needs to be kept firmly in hand, whereas, in fact, such commitment is potentially an excellent resource for the RE teacher. Of course some Christian teachers may be bigoted; so may teachers of any other subject. Bigotry remains bigotry whether it be of the atheist sort, socialist, Tory or whatever, and is to be deplored. However, where the Christian RE teacher is committed to an open approach he brings with him into the classroom a surer inner grasp of the shape and feel of his subject; he knows its proportions and relations in a way that a non-participant observer never can.

He also has a rich resource for understanding what it is to be a believer within another faith system than his own. John's practice is to invite to his classroom well-briefed Hindus and Jews so that his pupils meet real people whose lives are shaped by their deepest commitments. Listening to such visitors over many years; talking with them before their visit and meeting them socially has helped John increasingly recognise the seriousness and depth of 'other faiths'. While he does not share their beliefs and practices, his Christian experience has prepared him to recognise 'the holy' in the experience of others. He knows the power of that claim laid upon the believer by the transcendent; he recognises the ways in which religious language works, and more than a little of the place of sacred writings in the believer's life. For him, the richness and variety of worship is not a catalogue of odd things that believers get up to but a celebration — through ritual, symbol, story and personal response — of what matters most in the believer's life. When John talks with his Hindu visitors he is practising one of the most precious of human skills, one which he aims to share with his pupils, namely dialogue. In dialogue he listens carefully, allowing another to speak for himself. In dialogue he asks questions so that he can clarify for himself what the other is saying. In dialogue he will continue to exercise his critical skills and be prepared courteously to speak his own truth. His own religious experience will have helped him enter more surely into this dialogue and so into a way of teaching that can do nothing but good for his pupils; his commitment allows him to recognise and value the commitment of another.

It is precisely this insight which may now be seen as a resource for his teaching of the Christian tradition. Within the framework of his overall aim to bring about understanding in his pupils; within the context of trust naturally formed among students by his open approach; within his practice of dialogue, he may safely draw on his own experience to enrich his teaching. Naturally, he will carefully select what is appropriate. It is too easy to fall into the 'when I was in Poona' trap, even though where it is appropriate and positively contributes to a learning programme such personal experience is as much a resource as any visitor or video.

No one ceases to be himself when he sets out to help children learn, and his personal religious commitment can be one of the teacher's resources once he has grasped how it relates to his professional obligations. He is not neutral with respect to religious faith; the notion of neutrality too easily suggests unconcern with or indifference to faith — but he *knows* that it matters. But with his religious commitment he brings his professional commitment which ensures that he will respect the needs of his pupils, the expectations of his employers and be impartial in his treatment of others' religious commitments, taking off his shoes when he approaches another person's holy ground.

4 The political dimension of Christianity

David Minton

Christianity has a political dimension. A sound curriculum should involve learning about religion, and religion should encompass the study of Christianity, including its political dimension. This article aims to achieve an understanding and an interpretation of Christianity's political dimension and to communicate these to educationists, teachers, students, parents and others who are concerned with the matter. I certainly assume and envisage an educational context in which Political Education, along with Religious Education, is considered essential in schools. Political Education should be in the secondary school curriculum in its own right, either as a subject and department, or as an inter-departmental or cross-curricular undertaking, involving History, Geography, Environmental Studies, Economics, Religious Studies, World Studies and any other subject to which it is integral. Religious Studies should not be the only subject in which political education takes place, nor should Religious Studies ignore the political dimension of any religion that is studied.

Education has a political dimension. In a closed society this is to do with bringing up citizens to believe in and to serve the ideology of the state. In an open society it is to do with bringing up citizens to exercise their democratic rights with the maximum of information and integrity. Most societies have their open and closed aspects, but most can also be characterised as relatively open or relatively closed. There are societies with an apparently strong Christian connection in each of these two categories.

This ambiguity can be traced in part to a conflict between two functions which seem to be inherent in all religion. The first is the homoeostatic or conservative function, whereby religious traditions are among the most successful of all social structures in preserving the status quo. Religion can thus play a part in the more closed, totalitarian or authoritarian kind of society. The second function is the radical or reformative, or even revolutionary, whereby values and insights gained in religion have contributed to great improvements in social justice, human rights and welfare. Religion can thus play a part in the more open or liberal kind of society. This tension appears with particular sharpness in the case of Christianity. For example, William Wilberforce proposed the abolition of slavery on Christian grounds but Christian bishops in the House of Lords voted against the proposal. Again, Christianity was equally involved in the Civil Rights movement of Martin Luther King and in the white segregationism of the American South. Teaching about Christianity should certainly not include the reformers if it does not also include the reactionaries. Rather, it should encourage pupils to understand both.

Such an understanding can be reached by considering the two main strands in Christianity's political character, which can be called 'historical immanentism' and 'sapiential pragmatism',[1] both of which are evident in the Old Testament, the New Testament and the history of the Church. The difficult label of historical immanentism accurately identifies the dominant and overt dynamism of both Judaism and Christianity. Immanentism means that aspect of religious consciousness which senses God as 'dwelling within'. Without doubt biblical religion in general and Christianity in particular are both transcendentalist and immanentist, seeing God as not only above and beyond the universe but also as deeply within things. In all religions the immanentist sense of God includes the mystical, God being 'deep in the lotus of the heart' for the Hindu; 'closer to man than his jugular vein' for the Muslim; and 'Christ in you' for the Christian. What is central to, and distinctive of, biblical religion is that, in addition to this mystical immanence, there is also an historical immanence.

The indwelling presence of God, which is in a sense the Bible's principal theme, is not just in 'temples made with hands', or only in the heart of the individual. It is also in history. The Bible is a *Heilsgeschichte,* the 'sacred history' of God's activity from the Alpha of Creation to the Omega of the Last Day. The vehicle or firmament of Christianity (i.e. the medium through which revelation is both given and vindicated) is history. The covenant between God and Moses was about the history of a human collectivity, Israel. In other words, it was political. The basis of the covenant was what God *had* done, in leading the captives from Egypt, and the promise of the covenant was what God *would* do, saving the nation and making it central in history's final era of universal peace. The sanction of the covenant, what God would inflict on the chosen people if they were not faithful, was again historical and political, i.e. national disaster. History, defined as events and destinies concerning individuals and social groups such as nations, was *par excellence* the medium of God's purpose and activity in the religion of ancient Israel and the Old Testament. God was immanent within the historical process.

Related to this historical immanentism was the prophetic tradition. The great individual prophets, who broke the moulds of court soothsaying and corporate ecstasy, were God's spokesmen with an eye on history. They took the people to task for breaking the commandments of the covenant and pointed to contemporary or forthcoming events as indications of God's displeasure. The 'Thus saith the Lord' can be taken as referring not only to the prophets' words but also to the events in history of which they were an interpretation. Thus Israel's fluctuating fortunes and the rise and fall of surrounding empires were seen as the arena in which God's purpose was being worked out.

It might be thought that the elements of prophecy and historical immanentism are less evident in the New Testament, and that the Gospel of Jesus was apolitical. That would be to forget that the community of the old covenant, Israel, is replaced by the new community which acknowledges the rule of God in Christ, the Church. The picture of a society ruled by God in the Sermon on the Mount and the Parables of the Kingdom is strikingly political. It shows a community in a state of transformation, revolutionised by seemingly impossible ideals and mysteriously coming to fruition. Jesus was certainly no zealot, agitating and active in overthrowing a particular oppressor. He was, however, the initiator of a radical change in human and social values. His arrival in Jerusalem at the beginning of the Passover Week, with its intentional resonance of Old Testament kingship themes, had a political flavour, which was well conveyed, for example, by Pasolini in his memorable film, *The Gospel According to Saint Matthew*.

When in the subsequent history of Christianity attempts have been made to mould the political life of a community on the absolute imperatives in the teaching of Jesus, such as the Anabaptist commune in Münster and the Calvinistic theocracy in Geneva, the results have been dramatic. They have provoked the most acute hostility, not least from the mainstream Church. Meanwhile, through the centuries, large-scale Christian collectivities have continued the Old Testament tradition of seeing the hand of God in historical change and helping it by fighting holy wars. Thus, for example, to the conquests and tribulations of ancient Israel are added the Holy Roman Empire, the 'Christianising' of Iceland, and the Crusades. At the present time there are Christians deeply involved in the processes of revolution, such as the Roman Catholic priests who are shoulder-to-shoulder with Marxists in the struggle against authoritarian regimes in Latin America. Here the materialistic immanentism of the Marxist's dialectic finds common ground with the spiritual immanentism of his religious colleagues, for both agree that the present chapter of the story is wrong, even though they disagree as to how the plot finally unfolds.

The second and contrasting strand in the political character of Christianity is what can be called its 'sapiential pragmatism', going back to the Wisdom tradition of the Old Testament rather than the prophetic. It also has played its part at all stages in the formation and history of Christianity. It was this, perhaps, that dictated the Davidic and Solomonic synthesis, whereby the Children of Israel, in spite of the prophets, were allowed to follow the surrounding peoples so far in their style of government and religion as to have a king and a temple. This was also perhaps the spirit of such sayings of Jesus in the New Testament as, 'Render unto Caesar the things that are Caesar's and unto God the things that are God's',[2] 'Be ye as cunning as serpents and as harmless as doves'[3] and 'The children of this world are wiser in their generation than the children of light'.[4] It was in this spirit that Paul advised slaves to be obedient to their masters,[5] and spoke of being all things to all men; of doing as the Romans when in Rome.

History, since New Testament times, bears further witness to this pragmatic or opportunist element in Christianity. It was with the conversion of the Roman Emperor, Constantine, and the subsequent acceptance of Christianity as the official religion of the Roman Empire, that Christianity first joined the ruling class in politics. This raises the problem as to whether power in this world is compatible with the spirit of the Cross. Rule over the world's kingdoms was, after all, the lure of one of the temptations that Jesus rejected. Constantine's vision of the flaming cross with its motto *In hoc signo vinces,* (In this sign you will conquer), is as unacceptable to the Christian radical or idealist as it is acceptable to the Christian pragmatist. Christians in any political situation, as for example that of seventeenth-century England, seem to divide into three camps: those who accept the status quo and see divine right within it — the Cavaliers; those who seek to wrest power in order to use it for what they see as greater justice — the Roundheads; and those who change their colour and survive, whatever the circumstances — the Vicar of Bray, and others like him.

The conflict between the prophetic and the pragmatic is further explained by the idea of the 'dual citizenship' of the Christian. As was shown by St Paul, St John the Divine, and St Augustine, Christians are citizens of two cities — the earthly and the heavenly. In their earthly citizenship should Christians acquiesce in less than ideal social arrangements, believing that, although the earthly city will pass away, the heavenly city is eternal? Or should they strive for the ideals of the Sermon on the Mount, believing that they are colonising the earthly city for the sake of the heavenly city and that the kingdom of heaven is already among them? It is significant that the Greek, *entos humōn,* can be interpreted as either 'within you' or 'among you'.[6] Christians who emphasise that the kingdom of heaven is *'among* you' see the rule of God as something to be served externally through the institutions of the world. They seek to change the world through these institutions and, if necessary, to change the institutions, themselves. On the other hand, Christians who emphasise the *'within* you' see the role of God primarily as something inward and pietistic and tend to be more reactionary in political matters, or less political altogether.

This tension between the city of God and the human city leads to two other elements in the political character of Christianity, those of 'transformation' and 'eschatology'. By transformation I mean the process whereby the earthly city becomes more like the heavenly and the ideals of the latter become more evident in the realities of the former. The emancipation of slaves, the extension of human rights, universal suffrage, race desegregation and the liberation of women might all be said to be steps in the transformation of the human city in God's kingdom, not because the New Testament and Christian doctrine say much explicitly about such things, but because they follow from Jesus' basic principles of analogy and reciprocity — 'Love thy neighbour as thyself' and 'Do unto others as you would have them do unto you'.

A Christian, according to the New Testament, is a person transformed, or at least under transformation, and the Church is a community which is both transformed and transforming. Such a transformation is particularly evident in the teaching of the Sermon on the Mount and in the account of the first Churches in the book of Acts. The kingdom of God and politics are both a matter of Rule. The government of Christ should have a transforming effect on the government of the human race. The degree to which the transformation is an imperative or just a description is reflected in the differing degrees and directions of political activism among Christians. For example, Paul writes, 'There is neither Jew nor Greek, there is neither bond nor free, there is neither male nor female: for ye are all one in Christ Jesus.'[7] In one sense this can be taken as a *description*, i.e. a Christian just doesn't take any notice of these divisions which may be significant to some people. In another sense the sentiments expressed in this verse can be seen as a *prescription*, i.e. saying, 'As Christians you are to make sure that in the world there is no discrimination on the grounds of race, social position or sex.' In this latter sense the transformed life of the kingdom of God is a call to action, whereas in the former it is a change of attitude.

Whichever of the foregoing alternatives is the more authentic or the more Christian, there is no doubt that the political character of Christianity has an eschatological as well as a transformative element. Christianity is committed to a vision of an era in which the tranformation is consummated and when the rule of God is finally established in the world of men. Christians are divided as to whether the coming of God's kingdom will occur through historical processes or through supernatural and apocalyptic events. Here again the difference becomes a matter of degrees of activism. Do Christians work or wait for God's government of the world? On the one hand conservative Christians tend to wait, and on the other hand radical and revolutionary Christians work, perhaps even militantly.

Connected with the elements of transformation and eschatology is the question of means. How should Christians expect political change to arise in the world? By democracy? By persuasion? By revolution? By terror? By non-violence? Every one of these possibilities has been tried in the name of Christ, but which appears to be most clearly in the spirit of Christ? Here the teacher, or pupil, who is considering the political character of Christianity, has to decide for himself or herself as to which, for example, are nearer to the spirit of Christ: the Christian Democratic parties of Western Europe or the movements of Mahatma Gandhi and Martin Luther King?

The Christian who turns to the political map of the present-day world from the Sermon on the Mount and the Passion Narrative may be understandably bewildered. In the first place there is the capitalist bloc, with the strongest explicit link to Christianity, declaring a great emphasis on freedom and human rights, but operating an economic system which is not easily sustained from early Christian principles referring to the distribution of wealth.[8] In the second place, and equally anomalous, there is the communist bloc, apparently operating closed societies and denying human rights, and making a declaration of atheism, but proclaiming economic and social aims which comply with both the teaching of Jesus about responsibility for other people and the 'primitive communism' of the earliest Church. In the third place there is the Third World, emerging from colonisation and exploitation by Christian countries, but in large measure exhibiting an economic status *vis-à-vis* the first two worlds which some Christians would consider is materially the most comparable of the three with Jesus's teaching about suffering and service.

If the political character of Christianity exhibits the features mentioned so far in this sketch, there now remain inferences to be drawn concerning the curriculum and the classroom. I conclude by outlining five which seem to be of particular importance:

1. Study of the role of Christianity in political changes and conflicts, both past and present, should further the understanding of both Christianity and politics. The ambiguity and inconsistency, even the contradictions, of the Christian presence in politics renders such a study more, rather than less, important.

2. The political character of Christianity should be taught in the context of the political character of other religions. Just as in an increasingly secular and pluralistic society all the beliefs and structures of Christianity need to be taught in the context of the world's views of life and ways of life as a whole, so the relation between Christianity and politics needs to be studied with an eye to the relation between other religions and politics. It may well become evident in such a study that the political imperatives implicit in Christianity are, on the one hand, not as compelling or as homogeneous as those of Islam, for example, or, on the other hand, as muted or as diverse as those, for example, of Hinduism.

3. The relation between Christianity and politics needs to be presented as a cluster of concerns rather than as an agenda for action. The concerns may pull in different directions, even if they are not actually incompatible, but their very ambiguity and tension are at the very centre of the Christian inspiration.

4. The relation between Christianity and politics should be presented across the whole gamut of political contexts, from the global to the personal. Thus a complete picture in any course or syllabus would have to include the world-scene with its blocs and its areas of current conflict; the national scene, with its parties and issues; the local scene, often with its involvement of particular religious communities; and the individual scene with its politics of personal interaction and experience.

5. The relation between any religion and politics raises three questions, all of which must be pursued in the case of Christianity. The first is, 'What is the ideal political state of affairs envisaged by the religion?' The second is, 'What have been and are the actual effects of the religion on politics?' The third question is, 'What kind of politics exists within the religion's own organisation of itself – in its hierarchies, councils and decision-making?' Ideally all three questions should have the same answer, but Christians, like

members of all other religions and persuasions, are not entirely successful in practising what they preach, or indeed in preaching the same thing.

NOTES

1. *'Historical immanentism and sapiential pragmatism'*

These terms are not knowingly borrowed, but as labels for political currents in biblical religion represent coinages of my own. The thinking behind the former is much influenced by such writings as:
Erich Voegelin, *A New Science of Politics;*
Leo Strauss, *Natural Right and History;*
Mircea Eliade, *Cosmos and History;*
Karl Lowith, *Meaning in History.*

The basic idea of 'historical immanentism', which in all the above-mentioned works is regarded as most questionable, is that of a direct equation between historical events and the nature or will of ultimate reality — 'God', who is immanent not so much in the cosmos or nature ('how things *are*') but in the succession of events ('what *happens*') — i.e. assumptions of progress, dialectic, history 'delivering the goods' or even 'history delivering the good' (eschatology).

The label 'sapiential pragmatism' describes an important aspect in the political profile of the Judeo Christian tradition during and since the biblical period. It emphasises, on the one hand, the Wisdom tradition in ancient Hebrew religion, associated with the figure of Solomon and such sapiential writing as Proverbs and Ecclesiastes and, on the other, the practicality and opportunism associated with such figures as King David in the Old Testament and St Paul in the New.
For general reference refer to B.W. Anderson, *The Living World of the Old Testament.*
2. Matthew 22:21
3. Matthew 10:16
4. Luke 16:8
5. Ephesians 6:5 Colossians 3:22
6. Luke 17:21
7. Galatians 3:28
8. Acts 4:32−37

5 Christianity in its cultural contexts

Clive Erricker

My aim is to present a case for the need to understand Christianity within its different cultural contexts or settings. This is **not** offered as an all-embracing approach but one necessary aspect of the overall approach to understanding the subject, just as, for example, the study of biblical teachings is another.

THE TEACHER'S DILEMMA

It is hard to know how best to study and teach about a religious tradition, the spiritual ideal often seems to inhabit another plane from that which can be discovered anthropologically through observing the way each believer's faith is acted out in the everyday world. The two are difficult to integrate. This reveals itself in the classroom in simple, but baffling, encounters for teachers when their theological explanation of what Christians do is countered by a pupil saying that they know someone who goes to church down their road who isn't like that at all. I have been in the same sort of situation when inviting a Muslim student to talk to a group about his religion. He started by saying he wasn't really religious, but that didn't mean he wasn't a Muslim. What should one do? Does the teacher say that the particular example offered by the pupil is of someone who isn't a real Christian? Was my student not a real Muslim? Of course, we recognise the difference between people who are more or less devout, but this isn't really enough. If people wish to be accepted as adherents of a faith, to whatever degree and with whatever justification, then surely the student's and teacher's task is not first of all to make a judgement on them on theological grounds. Similarly, if a tradition counts amongst its faithful the majority of a population whose behaviour does not approximate to the teachings of the Sermon on the Mount or the Ten Commandments we cannot make an initial judgement on the way that institution claims its adherents. It is part of our study to acknowledge that it makes this claim or that individuals within traditions make certain claims, and then discover the reasons. If, in our judgement, incongruities are unearthed and paradoxes and contradictions emerge, so be it. We must start by saying that is in the nature of the things to be explained. Where the ideal, which is worked out theologically, and the actual, which is observed anthropologically, conflict, that area is something to explore with intellectual curiosity.

THE APPROACH: IMPLICIT RELIGION IN AMERICAN SOCIETY

What are the reasons for such conflict? First we must acknowledge that any religious ideal consists in statements that have no specific cultural context. I do not mean by this that the words of the Sermon on the Mount weren't voiced at a particular place and particular time. I mean they have come to be understood as that which should be striven for by all believers regardless of each one's situation. However, every tradition ceaselessly finds itself in different historical and cultural contexts. Whereas the ideal is atemporal, the actual is not. In short each believer is not simply a Christian but also has other allegiances in terms of nationality, politics and family circumstances, and also experiences constantly changing emotional, moral, economic and intellectual influences and tensions. When observing Christianity we are also observing this total experience at work. The study of the ideal has its own special value, but it is the map to be followed rather than the journey taken. Here we are concerned with the journey itself.

The relationship between a person's religious stance and the other factors that claim his allegiance is complex. For example, we know that to be Christian and British, for most people today, does not constitute a necessary or even expected combination. As a consequence public statements that presume the one and imply the other are relatively rare. The language of British nationalism and that of Christianity are usually distinct, though it was not always so.[1]

By contrast, if we look at the United States the same is not true. There is an interchangeable symbolism between the two languages so that one type of statement also serves as an example of the other. This emerges in the diverse contexts of public life. Consider the following remarks made by Miss America to the press after her enthronement:

'When the new Miss America met the Press, she said that God should never have been expelled from the classroom, that she followed the flag with her whole body and that she tried to live her Christian values seven days a week'. (*Observer*, 5 November 1984)

Thus the American flag embodies American values and Christian ones. The most obvious theological justification of her 'body' statement from the Christian point of view must be St Paul's understanding of the body as the temple of the Spirit in 1 Corinthians 8. Miss America probably did not consciously refer back to St Paul when she made this statement; rather it is an example of a Christian idea now being equally accepted as part of the language of American ethics. Miss America's Christianity is composed in this way. Of course, if one were cynical about Miss America's presentation of herself, this would not invalidate the above interpretation since she would still be expressing what is felt to be acceptable to the American people as a whole. In fact, one of the moral tensions of American society is brought out by comparing her to her predecessor whose crown was removed with embarrassment after she had posed for *Penthouse* magazine.

Another moral tension comes out in the following example from James Agee's record of his experience in the CIA.[2] He quotes a speech given by General Lemay on the theme of patriotism:

> Our patriotism must be intelligent patriotism. It has to go deeper than blind nationalism or shallow emotional patriotic fervour. We must continually study and understand the shifting tides of our world environment. Out of this understanding we must arrive at sound moral conclusions. And we must see to it that these conclusions are reflected in our public policies....If we maintain our faith in God, our love of freedom, and superior global air power, I think we can look to the future with confidence.

The speaker feels no incongruity when suggesting that faith in God, love of freedom and superior global air power go together and it is significant that he believes faith in God to be as important to the American way of life as the other two. If we believe such faith to be threatened by the evil of atheism, which is coupled with a disregard for freedom, as he clearly does, we arrive at a rationale for superior air power starting from a religious point of view. It is one way of conducting a just war, allied perhaps to an over-assertive attitude and sense of national pride, but nonetheless with a firmly held religious conviction.

Superior global air power may not appeal to us as a symbol for Christian faith but this may be more a question of sensibilities than ethics.[3] The association of faith and power can be expressed in other ways. In Victor Jara's poem 'Prayer to a Labourer' the themes of power, faith and freedom are again linked but with different political and cultural associations:

Stand up
Look at the mountain
Source of the wind, the sun, the water
You who change the course of rivers,
Who with the seed sows the flight of your soul.
Stand up
Look at your hands
Take your brother's hand so that you can grow
We'll go together united by blood.
The future can begin today.
Deliver us from the master who keeps us in misery.
Thy kingdom of justice and equality come.
Blow like the wind blows,
The wild flower of the mountain pass.
Clean the barrel of my gun like fire.
Thy will be done, at last on earth
Give us strength and courage to struggle.
Blow like the wind blows,
The wild flower of the mountain pass.
Clean the barrel of my gun like fire.
Stand up
Look at your hands

Take your brother's hand so you can grow,
We'll go together united by blood.
Now and in the hour of our death.
Amen.

Despite the commendation of Christian violence there is a feeling more of gentleness and less of aggression which may make it more palatable to religious sentiment generally. Nevertheless, true to the first principles of our approach we must simply observe the similarities at work and be aware of the differences. In so far as both are expressions of Christianity they differ in accordance with the social and cultural circumstances that have given rise to them. In each case the threat is different, as is the weaponry and the justification, but the response is similar: violent resistance. Significantly, Christianity in the first case is identified with a national way of life, and in the second with the brotherhood of oppressed humanity, and it is this kind of distinction that we have to be aware of in order to understand the variety of its expression in different cultural contexts.

THE APPROACH: MAINSTREAM TRADITIONS AND DISSENT

This characteristic doesn't only reveal itself in ethical and political pronouncements but in other dimensions of life which are specifically religious. In the following example from Ninian Smart's *The Phenomenon of Christianity*, he explains how it happens in ritual:

> The prestige of the Orthodox Church and its relative freedom under a Red administration stem in part from its historic role in the expression of Romanian identity, but it is also of a piece with so much of Eastern Christian history, living over long periods in captivity....
>
> As elsewhere in Orthodoxy, the sacred liturgy is the chief glory of the faith. Over three hours chanting, prayers and ceremonial might prove tedious; not so, for the whole thing is what it is often claimed to be − heavenly, and the three hours re-enactment of the Christian drama of redemption means something about survival.

These complex and culturally-related characteristics don't necessarily abide by denominational rules. Though Ninian Smart's example is the expression of a particular tradition, it is true that such traditions came into being through particular historical circumstances and those issues which were instrumental in their formation at the time may cease to have primacy at a later date. Equally, new issues may claim allegiance and new Christian movements may emerge and become institutionalised. It is common therefore to find the influence of Christianity in a society expressed through other than denominational channels focusing on issues that have no clear institutional dividing lines. The nuclear debate is one such issue today; the Church's response to political issues such as poverty and economic growth is another; and, as we have seen, the question of what constitutes the religious aspect of nationalism and morally healthy Americanism is a third.

Within this context the language of dissent is also formed. As a secular example, in John Huston's film *Wise Blood*, made in 1979, the hero, upon stealing a luxurious American sedan and making his way through the Bible belt of the southern states, expresses the materialist doctrine that 'A man with a good car ain't got no need to be justified'. I certainly believe there is some cynical truth in this statement but again it highlights the tensions in American morality between its implicit Christian influence, expressed in the notion of justification, and its overt materialism, of which the car is the symbol.

A religious example of dissent are the Amish communities living on small farms spread across the United States from Pennsylvania to Indiana. In denying themselves all luxuries their dissenting puritanism is most clearly expressed in their dress and appearance and their distrust of all technology. Their sectarian allegiance is so firm that they even run their own education system, often with ungraded one-room schools, and have a ban on higher education beyond the age of fourteen. It is difficult to find other Christian groups for whom technology and education are such central religious issues but in a study of their tradition in the context of American society it becomes clear why this is so.

The historical dimension of this approach can also be illustrated by pointing to the strong influence of Christianity on *British* society in the past. A clear mainstream example is the architecture of the Oxford and Cambridge colleges. Until the end of the nineteenth century they were constructed with the chapel and the dining hall as two of the central public areas, each sharing a remarkable similarity of design — long and lofty with seating arrangements down their length proceeding from the entrance at one end to the place of most importance and sacredness at the other. This reflects the hierarchical structure of a society supported by a mainstream Anglican tradition whose own organisation was of the same kind. Implicit in this are certain national beliefs in the way things ought to be ordered which are reflected in the denomination's teachings. Wedded to this are certain moral values reflected in the faces of the ordained past masters of the college hanging above the diners in the hall.[4] They express paternal benevolence, earnestness, studious absorption and diligence in turn. The ritual of the dining hall also reminds us of the antiquity of the spiritual foundation to civilised life in the Latin grace. The way in which its orderliness is maintained is reflected in the waiters who serve out the food to those at table. Amongst others, Selwyn College, Cambridge, provides a clear example of all these points. This mainstream expression of a particular type of Christianity is wedded to and underpins certain social values which can, by virtue of this outlook, be said to be Christian because they are endorsed by Christianity. This is expressed in the rituals, architecture, language and statutes of the institution. Consider the fact that F.D. Maurice could not receive his degree until he became an Anglican.

What is true of mainstream Christianity in the public institutions of a state is also true of dissenting bodies. The contrasting of Quaker ceremony and the language of Quaker belief merits investigation in the same way. My point is that unless we incorporate this approach into our teaching of Christianity it will not make much sense to pupils in the classroom. They will not understand how what they are aware of in the world around them, which they regard as largely or wholly secular, consists of a culture that is permeated with Christianity. Its influence exists in both the institutions and the outlook of individuals in their culture, whether overtly religious or not. Furthermore, since for pupils to make sense of themselves and their world we must all have an awareness of the cultural influence of religious tradition; the teaching of RE must be placed at the centre of the study of the Humanities.

PRACTICAL IMPLICATIONS FOR TEACHING CHRISTIANITY

One of our main objectives in teaching Christianity or any other religion is to explain the meaning of the faith for the believers.

In Ninian Smart's example of the liturgy of the Romanian Church this liturgy is an expression of the continuing survival of the people, as well as of their hope of final redemption. In a sense the redemption hope is being realised in the ritual re-enactment of their continuing experience. Redemption now takes on a meaning which can be understood through the lives and actions of particular people. It is no longer simply an abstract theological concept for the child. To put it bluntly, through being moved by the experience of others, the pupil will understand that which he cannot understand purely on the intellectual level. This seems to me to be faithful to what Christianity is actually about: a lived faith. Therefore we are looking at the right medium for the message.

Let us consider another example. What of the structure of the Oxbridge colleges or the Quaker meeting houses? How is this to be handled? Theologically they have different emphases, for like Gothic cathedrals, the long aisles and 'high tables' of the colleges point to God's majesty and his otherness from man. They also emphasise the ordering of the world by the creator for his creatures, from the lowest to the highest. Recognition of the natural order extends into the social order. God has ordered every man's estate, as the hymn tells us. At the same time there is something of Bunyan's road to the celestial city in this. From the entrance to the focus of the building is an ascent that each Christian citizen, and civilisation itself, is encouraged to make: a metaphor for redemption again. The Quaker emphasis is quite different; the hierarchical motif of the architecture and ritual has collapsed. This is a theological comment related to the question of relationships within society. Rather than otherness and order, we are encouraged to recognise God's approachability and man's unity and sameness before him. The story is told with its different accents reflected visually in the architecture and ritual of the particular institutions observed. This interpretative activity for pupils is the way they can come to understand why Christianity is represented in the ways it is. We have a concrete starting point in the phenomena of the civilisation we live in. A visit to a church, for example, can aim at illustrating the outlook of its adherents through its features. Each type of building is the story of Christianity interpreted in a different way.

What of the American general? The equation for a civilised life is freedom, faith in God and confidence in your military power to assert and defend what you stand for. When studying Christianity in the context of world affairs it is necessary to understand this equation in order to make sense of the strategies and activities of one country in relation to other countries. This is borne out by the confrontations that have taken place between United States' policy and the government of Nicaragua or the Liberation theologians in Latin America. The correspondence between Archbishop Oscar Romero of San Salvador and

President Carter, and the latter's eventual re-intensification of military activity and government aid in El Salvador, bears witness to why the above equation is an important one for the United States. This face of Christianity is also an important one to understand in order to make sense of international affairs, in the context of World Studies as well as Religious Education[5].

I hope the above examples go some way towards exemplifying the value of the approach commended in this article to classroom teaching.

NOTES

1.   Of course, the identification of Christian values with those of British society is still made. In *The Times* leader of 1 April 1985 entitled 'In Holy Week' we read 'The two major public periods, those spanning Christmas and Easter, are repeated annual demonstrations that important events in the Christian calendar are important events still in the life of the nation.' The writer then goes on to explain how Jesus still represents the perfect humanity to be imitated. However this is no longer reflected in a major way in institutional life. Church membership is low and attendance is lower. School assemblies, the one corporate expression within educational institutions indicative of their underlying attitudes, have less and less overt Christian content. Nevertheless it is evident that the notion of Christian virtue is still identified with the mores of some social groups. Indeed observing how this comes to be the case is the sort of enquiry I believe necessary to fully understanding the expressions of Christianity, which is what this paper has been concerned with.

2.   Agee, J. (1975) *CIA Diary*, Harmondsworth, Penguin Books, p.14.

3.   Compare the following claim in a TV advertisement for an American food processor: 'It can do the same things as any other food processor but being American it can do it with a little more muscle.'

4.   For a penetrating analysis of the social function of the oil painting generally and how that function has been inherited by advertising today consult – John Berger's *Ways of Seeing*, London, BBC Publications, 1972.

5.   This issue is dealt with in the final chapter of *Christian Ethics* in the Chichester Project series of textbooks on Christianity as a World Religion, Cambridge, Lutterworth Press, 1984.

SECTION B
ASPECTS

6 Jesus

Trevor Shannon

Many an RE teacher, on taking up a new post, has been confronted with the problem of having to teach a syllabus which he or she has not covered at college or university. It might be Wisdom Literature, the Oxford Movement, Buddhism, Sikhism or a whole host of other topics. It is a daunting but not insuperable problem. It involves a great deal of hard work but it brings with it distinct advantages. You start with a clean sheet and an open mind. You can read the scholarly books with a view to selecting and shaping and using the material in class. You can think about method as well as about content from the very beginning.

On the other hand there can be few, if any, RE teachers who come to the teaching about Jesus without previous knowledge and with a completely open mind.

In this article I wish to consider some of the implications of this almost unique situation in RE teaching: the advantages and the disadvantages.

In a school in which different religions, along with agnosticism and atheism, jostle each other our pupils sooner or later ask, belligerently or wearily, why we have to do so much about Jesus. Even if our syllabus is eminently well-balanced and enlightened we are, nevertheless, likely to feel there is some force in the question, and so I first consider why Jesus should take so prominent a place in our teaching.

THE IMPACT OF JESUS

I can say that if we teach about Christianity we cannot escape the centrality of the person of Jesus. Whatever sort of Christianity is looked at, Jesus dominates: he is the focal point of divergent Christian traditions. Christianity, its beliefs, its history and its worship cannot be understood without an understanding of Jesus.

We teach about Jesus because of his sheer historical impact and the impact of beliefs about him. Whatever the theological understanding of Jesus, it cannot be denied that faith in him and beliefs about him have had enormous historical consequences. Whether the consequences are good or bad may be debated; it cannot be debated that they are important. Wars, as any RE teacher is told by his or her pupils, have been fought in the name of Jesus and unspeakable atrocities committed in his name. Also in his name have been written some of the greatest works of literature. Jesus has inspired the building of Chartres, Salisbury, Milan and Coventry cathedrals. Great art has been inspired by the story or the person of Jesus. The masses, the passions, the oratorios and much other music have been created because of Jesus. All this is reason enough to study him.

Teaching about Jesus is inescapable because of the fascination that the figure of Jesus exercises. Habitually people clothe him in the dress of their own needs and concerns. In declining Imperial Rome he was seen as the pantocrator, the ruler of all. At other times he has been the exemplar of the monk, the man for others, the pre-eminently free man. He has been the teacher of situation ethics, the freedom fighter and political revolutionary. He has been the hippy Jesus of the flower people and the pacifist Jesus of Christian CND. Multi-faceted, fascinating — how can we avoid teaching about him?

As we begin the unavoidable task of teaching about Jesus, we must examine our presuppositions and those of our pupils. Problems which are simply part of the lot of the RE teacher by reason of the nature of the subject seem to be sharper and more clearly in focus in teaching about Jesus.

PROBLEMS WHEN TEACHING ABOUT JESUS

Scepticism

Christianity is, and for many years has been, a self-critical religion. Its self-criticism and questioning have been made public property by the media and the general public is aware of the uncertainties and differences of opinion within Christianity. What was the case with Colenso and Henson is more obviously the case with Jenkins, Cupitt, Küng and Schillebeeckx. Christianity questions itself in public and so it gets questioned. This contributes to the healthy scepticism and questioning which we find in pupils.

Not so healthy is the legacy of the post-Darwinian suspicion of religion. The idea that somehow science had discredited or disproved religion dies hard. No RE teacher can escape this. The resurgence of biblical fundamentalism (alongside a similar fundamentalism in Islam and, some would say, Judaism) makes the teacher's task of opening minds and following wherever truth may lead all the more vital.

We cannot overstress the depth and importance of this scepticism. I thought I was aware of it, but recall being told very sharply by some PGCE students that 11 year olds would not believe that Jesus existed at all unless I could prove it. That is healthy enough. It forces us to be thorough and honest in our teaching and reminds us that we cannot trade on received assumptions and easy answers. I shall return to this point later.

Scholarship

The second problem and opportunity for the teacher is the matter of scholarship. It is the practical problem for the working teacher of keeping up and doing justice to the continual advances in scholarship. How does the teacher select, study, understand and assimilate into everyday teaching this vast resource? There is no simple answer. Or rather, there is and it is simply hard work. One of the prime marks of the good teacher is that he or she is still reading five, ten, twenty, or thirty years after the completion of initial training. It means the discipline of reading a periodical that will direct you to what is worthwhile, and the acceptance of the simple truth that you cannot go on giving out unless you take something in. Freshness is vital and the yellowing pages of college notes should be burned, or at the very least looked upon with the greatest suspicion.

The vast resource of modern scholarship can either be viewed as a virtually unscalable mountain, daunting and frightening in its challenge, or as a quarry from which you can dig out information, incentive, interest and inspiration.

Commitment

A third and sensitive problem area is that of commitment. There is a growing number of RE teachers who are committed to RE but it remains true that the majority of RE teachers in the United Kingdom would call themselves Christians. The problem, therefore, is to be fair. We acknowledge that education, not evangelism, is the business of the classroom. We try not to suggest explicitly, or implicitly, that our beliefs are the only right ones, or the only ones worthy of serious consideration.

In recent years a great deal has been said and written about commitment, and while the problem is there for a Christian teaching anything about Christianity, it is at its most acute in teaching about Jesus. It is, however, in the nature of the job that we cannot stop and wait until we have sorted out our dilemma. The bell rings and we must go in the classroom and get on with it. What thought I have been able to give to the question leads me to believe that in the end I count Christian commitment an advantage in teaching about Jesus. I check this by analogy with other religious leaders and adherents of their faith. A practising Buddhist must have a greater insight about the Lord Buddha than a Christian. He or she will be able to teach about the Buddha with greater sensitivity than a Christian. They will be able to answer questions which are beyond the scope of a teacher looking at Buddhism from the outside.

The same must be true of the Christian teacher teaching about Jesus. That we have to be cautious and self-critical goes without saying, but bearing that in mind we should be ready to make the most of the advantage of reading and understanding as a believer, the documents which were written by believers for believers.

Pupil familiarity

A fourth problem or consideration is pupils' familiarity with the story of Jesus. Even if our society and our classes are religiously and culturally mixed, most children have heard about Jesus, often in an inaccurate or distorted way. The Easter holiday is the season for television to show Jesus films. *King of Kings* vies with *The Sound of Music* for the award for most regular showing. Jewish and Muslim children are as addicted to television as others and they all return to school not sure whether Christians think the Messiah was Jesus or Spartacus, Kirk Douglas or Don Cupitt.

When we teach about Jesus we have to reckon with the preconceptions and the part truths. Perhaps the most important thing we have to do is to break the stereotypes and let our pupils discover for themselves the awkwardness, the fascination and the multi-faceted nature of Jesus.

APPROACHES TO TEACHING ABOUT JESUS

The Jesus of history

The most formidable stereotype is that of our approach to teaching about Jesus. It might be argued that most of the problems outlined above derive from our preoccupation with the biblical—historical approach to Jesus. Many RE teachers have been trained in the liberal Protestant tradition with its emphasis on the careful, reverent study of the biblical texts. It is not surprising, therefore, that Agreed Syllabuses, teachers, books and GCE, CSE and proposals for the new combined 16+ examinations concentrate on this approach. The admirable *Hampshire Teachers' Handbook,* for example, clinging to this approach, suggests six areas that should be covered in teaching about Jesus — Jesus the Jew, concern for the poor and outcast, the man who was loved and hated, Jesus the teacher, puzzling stories, crucifixion and resurrection. All these concentrate on the Jesus of history, the Jesus of the Gospels, the Jesus of liberal Protestant scholarship. I should certainly not want to lose this approach. I believe that it is not only a valid way of approaching the person of Jesus, but that it can be an exciting and enlightening one for teachers and pupils alike.

The paths of this approach are well-trodden and one might justifiably ask whether new approaches are required. I am suspicious of simply watering down what the universities teach. I also have reservations about depending too much on the practice of checking what one can, and should, say about Jesus by reference to the Buddha or to Muhammad. I have tried another model: simply finding a historical character, in whom I have an interest, and seeing where the parallels might lead. I have chosen John Henry Newman.

If I want to teach you something about Newman it seems to me there are certain things you must know — certain areas I must cover.
1. You will not comprehend anything about Newman unless you are aware of the

historical context — the early-nineteenth-century reaction against liberalism in Church and state, the vestiges of fear of the revolution that had convulsed France, and the revival of serious or vital religion in the Evangelical Movement. You need to know about Oxford in the 1830s and 1840s. One requirement, therefore (note, not necessarily the first) is *historical context*.

2. You will also need to know something of the man himself and his background. I do not think it is necessary to know when he was born. You would need to know of his evangelical upbringing and the fact that he claimed that throughout his life he was sure of only two things — his own existence and that of God. So you need to know about his personal *background and character*.

3. You will need to know *what he did* — the charismatic magnetism of his character that caused young men in Oxford to copy the way he walked and the way he crashed to his knees in prayer. You will need to know what friends recorded of private conversations and what he said, devastatingly, in sermons. You will need to know of the tracts he wrote, his essays, his doctrinal and controversial articles and books.

4. You will need to know of his *ability to fascinate and repel*, his ability to make both friends and enemies, the passions he aroused, the controversies he fought and caused.

5. You will need to know about, and if possible feel, the tension, pressure and the sadness of what Newman called his *'death-bed period'* in the Church of England, his time at Littlemore, culminating in his leaving the Church of England and being received into the Church of Rome.

6. To be comprehensive you would need also to know about *his later life*, his life as a Roman Catholic (far longer than that in the Church of England), his loneliness, his holiness, his founding of the Oratory, his books, his poems, and his being made cardinal.

7. And finally we could consider his *influence*, both on his contemporaries and his lasting influence: I should say minimal, on the Roman Church, but profound and lasting on the Church of England.

That is just a grid, not a map. You could, I believe, start anywhere. You might start from the historical situation — or wherever you like.

Now apply the case of Jesus. If we remove the details we are left with a series of headings, most of which are usable and, I think, valid. The Religious Education teacher is more than capable of filling out the details, knowing that a fair approach has been made to understanding the historical Jesus.

The Christ of faith

It must, however, be conceded that the quest for the historical Jesus and the stimulating work of Cupitt, Nineham, Schillebeeckx and others means little and matters less to the majority of Christians in the world. For most Christians in Europe and North America as well as for those in Africa and Latin America, it is the Jesus of Christian worship, the Christ of the Church, who matters. I have recently asked many teachers if they try to teach about the Christ of Christian worship or the Christ of faith as opposed to the historical Jesus and their answers are a comforting echo of my own — No.

I shall try, therefore, to outline some of the ways in which I am trying to find a way into this approach. I realise, of course, that there must be many teachers who are already doing this and doing it well. But I know there are a sufficient number in a similar situation to me.

I hope the next few lines may be of help or stimulation to them.

Iconography

The New Testament's lack of interest in the physical appearance of Jesus has allowed artists to portray him as they wish. Apart from what seems to have been an 'official portrait' in the Byzantine and early medieval Church there have been as many faces of Christ as portrayers of him. Some have tried to depict the humanity of Jesus, others his divinity. Negro artists have often depicted him as a Negro and the Chinese as a Chinaman. What can be learned from these rather obvious observations?

Firstly, and simply, that for Christians it is not the appearance of Jesus that is important but who he was or might have been; what he said and did.

Secondly, we can consider if it is valid or why it is valid for Jesus to be depicted as a Negro or an Anglo-Saxon. I have met few teachers who cannot draw lessons out of a black Christ. But is it valid to extend the exercise and portray the crucified Jesus as a woman, as has been done recently by Julian Schnabel in New York?

We might go on and ask whether the various portrayals of Jesus in art are the visual equivalent to the way in which Christians down the ages have made Jesus into their own sectional image.

Jesus on crosses in churches, Jesus in stained glass windows and Jesus in some of the greatest art of the world: here is a resource for teaching that starts far away from our usual liberal Protestant approach but is just as much the Christ of the Christian Church.

One brief example of the use of iconography might be helpful. We shall consider two contrasting crucifixes: one a familiar Western crucifix bearing the dead Jesus (Picture 1), the other a 'Christus Victor' crucifix (Picture 2).

It would, of course, be preferable to have examples of the crucifixes in the classroom, or perhaps a local church would allow a visit so that they can be seen in their architectural and liturgical context.

(a) Pupils could be asked to look carefully at the crucifixes and then allocate to each words from a list. The list might contain the following: suffering, strong, defeated, weary, royal, human, priestly, calm, dead, beautiful, frightening, etc.

(b) Discussion, either as a class or in groups, could bring out the differences, such as crown of thorns and royal crown, clothed and naked, slumped and upright.

(c) Pupils can then suggest what each crucifix reveals about Christian beliefs about Jesus, e.g. one crucifix shows that they believe he was human and suffered and died a particularly unpleasant death. The other reveals that Christians do not regard the suffering and death as defeat. Careful questions about the figure and its clothes can reveal that for Christians Jesus is in some sense a king.

(d) Further consideration of crucifixes can bring out more aspects of Christian

*Picture 1   The Crucifixion by Graham
          Sutherland (Picture by courtesy
          of Cosmopress)*

Picture 2   Christus Victor by Mark Donaghue

(d) Further consideration of crucifixes can bring out more aspects of Christian belief about Jesus. For example, the way crucifixes are used: in homes where the Christian family eats together, what does the presence of a crucifix suggest?; at the roadside in traditionally Christian (particularly Roman Catholic) countries, what does that suggest?; at a bedside where prayers are said, how can that help the person who prays?

Depending on the group more sophisticated questions could be considered: would a crucifix remind or convince Christians of their belief in the living presence of Jesus? What feelings would a crucifix arouse? — fear? awe? gratitude? Could it limit Christians' idea of Jesus?

Ritual acts

This approach is more obviously interesting and I have never known it fail to arouse interest in pupils or teachers. I am suggesting an exploration of the 'body language' of the Church. I was brought up to bow my head when Jesus is named in the Creed. I recall standing in Church behind a lady whose habit it was to 'bob' or curtsy at the name of Jesus in hymns and prayers. More obviously the genuflexion before the sacrament in some churches says something powerful about beliefs about Jesus. The prostration before the cross on Good Friday in some traditions; the very powerful visual image in the TV film *The Thorn Birds* when before ordination the ordinand stretched himself, face down, in the shape of a cross, before the altar; processions bearing the image of Christ, or the sacrament of his presence; the cross carried through the streets on Good Friday — these are again powerful visual images, the physical articulation of beliefs. From these images pupils can be helped to discover Christian beliefs about and attitudes to Jesus.

These are some of the ways the Jesus of the Christian Church can be explored. By using art and ritual acts as well as the traditional liberal Protestant approach, we should gain a broader view of Jesus as the focal point of divergent Christian traditions, the centre point where all branches of Christianity meet.

7 The Bible

Peter Curtis

APPROACHING THE BIBLE: WHAT ARE OUR AIMS?

Few issues associated with Religious Education in schools have been discussed more frequently or with more vigour than the place of the Bible in the class-room. Virtually all RE teachers do some biblical work in the course of their teaching and so will have developed either consciously or unconsciously a stance on this issue. Any new discussion therefore takes place not in a vacuum but against a background of debate (much of it forcefully engaged in) and opinion (much of it strongly held). It is a valuable exercise for any teacher to stop from time to time to review his or her own stance. I suggest two ways in which this might be done, and it would be advantageous to try one (or both) before reading on.

Method one

Attempt to produce a list of goals that you would wish a child to achieve in terms of his or her study of the Bible by the time he or she completed his or her third year of secondary schooling. Analyse these into:

(a) knowledge gained;
(b) skills developed; and
(c) attitudes formed.

Method two

Read the following possible aims for biblical study in schools and decide how appropriate you consider each to be. Then review your own present teaching and, where appropriate, consider what degree of priority your present teaching attaches to each.

That pupils shall:

(a) become familiar with the broad outline of the Bible 'story' (i.e. Abraham – Paul);

(b) become familiar with selected key people and events in the Bible (e.g. Moses and the Exodus, the Covenant, Elijah, Amos, Jesus' ministry and teaching, Paul);

(c) examine the life and teaching of Jesus and be able to place him in his historical, cultural and religious context;

(d) be able to recite a number of selected passages of the Bible from memory;

(e) discover the many different types of literature that the Bible contains and appreciate the significance of literary type for a proper understanding of biblical material;

(f) have an opportunity to discover and express their own attitudes to the Bible;

(g) be able to learn and practise the skill of finding their way around the Bible (i.e. books, chapters, verses);

(h) come to acknowledge that the Bible contains a revelation of the nature of God and of his will for men;

(i) respect the Bible for the place it holds within the Christian religion;

(j) understand how the books of the Bible were written;

(k) understand the process of selection that resulted in the formation of the canon of biblical books;

(l) explore the use Christians make of the Bible in public worship and private devotion;

(m) appreciate the variety of ways in which Christians view the Bible and in particular the question of its authority;

(n) recognise that the English Bible is a translation from other languages and appreciate some of the principles and problems involved in the process of translation;

(o) know something of the history of the Bible in English and of the modern English translations of the Bible;

(p) be introduced to the fact of and methods of biblical criticism (as far as their age and ability permit).

THE USE OF THE BIBLE: WHAT IS ITS VALUE FOR CHRISTIANS?

The fact that there remains a great diversity of opinion and practice in itself justifies the attempt to explore further the use of the Bible in the classroom and to clarify some of the issues involved.

One use to which the Bible is sometimes put is that of a 'quarry' for material to illustrate themes and topics (courage, journeys, religious founders, etc.). Such a use, however, will not convey any appreciation of the nature of the Bible 'as a whole'. It will at the most provide fragmentary insights, odd pieces of a puzzle but no overall picture. The principal justification for engaging in a broader, more systematic study lies in the fact that some understanding of the Bible is essential to any understanding of Christianity as a whole, and no one, I imagine, would wish to dispute that this is a legitimate part of non-confessional RE even in a multi-faith Britain.[1] The Bible is the sacred book of the

Christian faith. It contains the fullest near-contemporary accounts of the actions and teaching of its founder. It contains the earliest attempts to understand the significance of Jesus. It contains the writings that throughout Christian history have been accepted by Christians as providing the norm for rules of behaviour and patterns of belief. It is read in almost every act of Christian worship. It has an authority for Christians beyond that of any other religious literature. It is the one collection of writings that Christians are prepared to speak of as the 'word of God'. Some understanding of its content and use is therefore an essential part of any attempt to understand the broader field of Christianity as a major world faith.

This justification has implications for syllabus content. The study of the Bible would not now be limited to contents but would include also a consideration of the place that the Bible holds within the Christian faith. Aims (i), (l), (m) and possibly (k) (see p.48) should become considerably more significant than they are in most current syllabuses. It becomes important for pupils to appreciate not only that the Bible is the Christian sacred book but also what that implies in terms of its use in public and private devotion and its role within the faith as a whole. When is the Bible read? By whom? Why? What is a lectionary and what is its purpose? Why do Christians read from both Old and New Testaments? What is the significance of the word 'testament'? What 'favourite' passages are there and why are they so popular? What biblical material is appropriate to any particular time in the Christian year? Why are there so many different translations? And so on. The questions are many. Here, however, we wish to enter a special plea for some serious consideration by pupils of the question of the authority of the Bible for Christians. It is not sufficient merely to introduce the idea of a 'canon' of scripture, a list of authoritative books. Exploring the ways in which the Bible is authoritative for Christians — the ways in which it is seen to be different from other religious literature — is an important part of the study. And we deliberately say 'ways' rather than 'way', for not all Christians have the same view of the Bible's authority and pupils should be aware of that fact. We oversimplify and thus fail to do justice to education or to Christianity if we suggest that all Christians are of the same mind on this issue. For example the 'fundamentalist' view of scripture is one approach and it is important that pupils should know of it. However, it would be wrong to give pupils the impression that all Christians are fundamentalists, that to be a Christian is to take the Bible literally and that if you cannot do so you cannot be a Christian. If one of the goals of RE is to help pupils develop a mature understanding of the major religious faith of this country we owe it to them to describe the broader, more complex situation that actually exists. While the stories of Wyclif, Tyndale, Coverdale and even Mary Jones that so frequently appear in school RE syllabuses are dramatic, and no doubt will continue to have their place, they are, I suggest, less urgent in terms of understanding Christianity today than the issue of authority.

THE CONTENT OF THE BIBLE –
NOT JUST A BOOK BUT A LIBRARY

Changes that have taken place in the RE world in the last two decades mean that

that the time available for the study of the content of the Bible will be considerably less than in previous years. The crucial task for the teacher, therefore, is to identify some helpful criteria for selection. Clearly it will not do just to recount the 'story' from Abraham to Paul. Nor will it be acceptable simply to study the Gospels. The Bible is not just a history; nor is it a life of Jesus. Neither does justice to the fuller picture. Reference to 'history' and 'Gospel' does, however, suggest one possible method of selection and one which we would wish to see taken more seriously than it is.

It is nothing new, of course, to see references in syllabuses to 'the Bible as a library'; this is a standard way of introducing even quite young pupils to the idea of the Bible as a composite work. It enables the teacher to introduce not only the idea of many books in one, but also that of multiple authorship and of composition spanning many centuries. It prepares the way for the concept of a 'canon' of scripture and thus for the question of authority discussed above. All of this suggests that it is a helpful way of introducing the Bible, in all its variety, to pupils. Sometimes this approach develops into an exploration of the fact that the Bible, like a library, contains a mixture of different types of literature.[2] Sadly, however, this is not always the approach and certainly it is not always made in any depth. I say 'sadly', for does not all sound understanding of literature rest upon a recognition and appreciation of literary type? It is only when we know what type of literature we are reading that we can know what expectations we should or should not have. It is only then that we know with what assumptions we should approach it and what questions it is legitimate to ask of it. In the interests of detachment we may illustrate this point with a non-biblical example. The works of the French fabulist, La Fontaine, are familiar to many. In one of his fables, 'The frog and the ox', a frog, seeking to emulate the size of the ox, puffs herself up, enquiring of her sister at various stages whether she has yet achieved her goal, until eventually she bursts. If on reading this story we were to ask 'Does this story provide evidence of a French species of speaking frog?' or 'Does this story suggest that an occasional cause of death among French frogs is self-inflation?' we should, of course, be foolish in the extreme. That is because this is an inappropriate type of question to ask of a fable. Such questions might conceivably be appropriate if we were reading the notebook of an explorer in previously uncharted forests, but they are not appropriate for fable. Of fable we have different expectations. When we read them we do so with different assumptions. So we ask 'What is the writer trying to say through this story?' or 'What is the moral of the story?' or 'Whom is the author satirising in this story?' Such questions are appropriate.

This, of course, is an extreme example but it serves to illustrate our point. As with fable, so with all the types of literature contained in the Bible (history, legend, myth, gospel, letters, laws, etc.) sound understanding rests upon recognition of the literary type. Many of the disagreements Christians have amongst themselves concerning the interpretation of the Bible stem from a failure to agree on what the literary type is and therefore what questions are appropriate. Much of the 'science versus religion' debate that was so intense in former years and which rumbles on in various ways has its origin in a similar confusion. And, if I may be permitted one less objective claim, much of the nonsense that is talked about the Bible today arises from a failure to take the multiplicity of literary types sufficiently seriously.

Not only then can the 'Bible as a library' approach introduce important insights into the Bible's composite nature, it can also lay the foundation for a sounder understanding of individual books and passages. But in addition (as hinted above − see p.50), it can help with the important but difficult task of selection. We have said above that teachers who limit themselves to the historical material or to the Gospels cannot be said to be introducing pupils to the Bible as such. That is, quite simply, because the Bible contains so much more than history or Gospel. It would be a useful exercise for any teacher to attempt to compile a list of the types of writing the Bible contains. The task, of course, is not a simple one. This is partly because literary categories overlap − much prophetic writing, for example, is also poetry − and partly because not all material is easy to categorise. Categories such as history, biography, legend, saga or epic might all be suggested for the Patriarchal Narratives. In addition, different theological stances colour our judgement of literary types. Some, for example, would resist any suggestion that books like Genesis or Jonah are not historical. Here, as in the more general issue of the place of the Bible in the classroom with which we began, it is important for teachers to recognise their own position and what the range of views is. They must also ensure that their pupils are similarly informed, for to press an individual viewpoint without acknowledging others is to be guilty of that charge of indoctrination which is so mistakenly levelled from time to time at RE in general. The task may be difficult, but certain categories would appear on most people's list − history, gospels, laws, letters, stories, prophecy and poetry, for example. Others might appear from time to time − legends, current affairs, myths, biography, autobiography, saga, allegories, apocalyptic visions, proverbs, 'Wisdom Literature', sermons and so on. It is not our claim that pupils must be introduced to every type of literature, but that an introduction to each of the major types will bring about a more balanced picture of what the Bible is than, for example, a purely historical study. In this way a study of literary type may assist with our task of selection. We end, therefore, with some observations concerning some of the major types of biblical literature and the ways in which they may be handled with pupils in the secondary school.

History

The historians of the Bible write with unconcealed assumptions. They assume that God exists, that he is in control of history, and the Israelites (and, in the case of the New Testament, the first Christians) are his chosen people. They write 'from faith'. So if the teacher presents the historical material from the Bible 'in its own words' and without comment or explanation, these assumptions may very easily result in teaching of a thoroughly confessional nature, only now it will be the Bible's faith rather than that of the teacher or syllabus-maker that will be stamped on the lessons. One way of avoiding confessionalism is to try to retell the Bible's story 'objectively', i.e. divested of its assumptions. But that, of course, would be to produce something quite different from the Bible's history which is not 'objective' but rather thoroughly 'committed'. Better then by far to recognise the nature of biblical history and to encourage pupils similarly to recognise it. Let the study of the Bible's history include a study of the assumptions and motives of the historians themselves. That way pupils are receiving a more genuine insight into the nature of this aspect of the literature of the Bible than they would from an objective study of the history of Israel and of the early Church.

Patriarchal Narratives

The problem of classifying these narratives into a literary category has already been mentioned. Here we note that the same pitfalls confront the teacher in handling this material as in handling biblical history. The goal must not simply be for pupils to 'know the story' but rather that they should understand the role the stories played and thus recognise why they were (and are) important to the Jewish people — note the Old Testament description of God as 'the God of our fathers, of Abraham, of Isaac, and of Jacob'. If pupils are enabled to appreciate these narratives as carriers of the essential concept of Israel as a covenant people from their very origins (as well, of course, as providing an explanation of how the people of Israel came to be in Egypt), justice will have been done to the biblical narratives as such.

Gospel

Gospel must be considered as a distinct literary type. Gospels are not the same as biographies and pupils should be helped to appreciate the differences. Once they know the meaning of the word 'gospel' and recognise its 'evangelistic' purpose (see Mark 1:1, John 20:30−31) they can begin to understand its distinct literary nature. The evangelists are no more objective than the Bible's historians. Their task is not to describe but to commend. All too frequently we 'lift' passages from the Gospels and use them to illustrate 'the historical Jesus' without a thought for the evangelical context from which they have been plucked. A part of the teacher's task is to help pupils understand the nature of 'gospel'. Such is a prerequisite for the study of any one Gospel's presentation of Jesus.

Poetry

Few pupils recognise how extensive poetry is in the Bible, found, as it is, not just in the Book of Psalms, but in the works of the prophets, on the lips of Jesus, and in many places elsewhere. The teacher's main concern will be with the skills of interpretation and thus the exploration of the poet's mind and feelings. From a study of selected psalms pupils can learn much of Hebrew belief and worship (sometimes at particular points in Israel's history — see

Psalm 137), as well, of course, as discovering something of the unique nature of Hebrew poetry.

Prophecy

Let us begin by eschewing certain goals, e.g. to demonstrate that the prophets look forward to the coming of Jesus. Such a view of the prophets belongs to the community of Christian belief. By all means let pupils know that many Christians so understand the prophets of the Old Testament, but our major concern with them must be to illustrate the role they played within the history of Israel, seeking to keep people true to the covenant with God and offering an interpretation of history in the light of their religious convictions. It is not necessary for pupils to read all the prophets − not even all the major ones. What is important is that sufficient examples should be introduced to build up a picture of the type of figures the prophets were and thus to distinguish them sharply from fortune-tellers, palmists, crystal-ball gazers and the like. To use a traditional distinction, it is important that pupils recognise the prophets as 'forth-tellers' as well as 'foretellers'.

Stories

This category sounds rather vague and is deliberately so. But it is helpful in that into it we may, with due caution, place the story-parables of Jesus, much of the material of Genesis 1-12, and longer works like the Book of Jonah and parts of the Book of Daniel. Our concern here, remembering what was said about La Fontaine's fable, is to ensure that pupils are asking the appropriate questions. Let the pupil ask, first of all, what meaning the story has, rather than whether the story is 'true'. While it is quite proper for pupils to be aware that there are Christians who believe the story of Jonah literally, it is more constructive for us as educators to invite pupils to reflect on the story's meaning rather than the digestive processes of 'great fish'.

It is not possible within the space of one brief discussion to raise all the questions that arise from the issue of the place of the Bible in the classroom, let alone to answer them. But if this discussion has raised some pertinent questions and suggested some possible answers it will have served its purpose.

NOTES

1. This is not to rule out other possible justifications. For example, within the context of the study of Judaism, the Old Testament (not, of course, so called in that context) will be studied as Jewish sacred scripture.

2. See the helpful discussion in Dale, A.T. (1972) *The Bible in the Classroom*, Oxford, Oxford University Press.

8 Christian worship
John Rankin

WORSHIP AS THE 'WAY IN'

It has frequently been said that religious concepts are too difficult for children to understand. Sometimes this is given as a reason why it is inappropriate to teach Buddhism or Hinduism or some other religion. Goldman demonstrated (*Religious Thinking from Childhood to Adolescence,* 1965) that what were often assumed to be simple Christian concepts caused problems for children. Goldman's work is no longer considered able to bear all the conclusions he drew from it, but it is certainly true that the 'propositions' of a religion are not the best route for children to gain an understanding of it. Indeed, it is probable that it is not the best route for most adults either. It is more appropriate to direct attention to the concrete manifestations of religion, to what people *do.* In the case of Christianity, teachers have felt this instinctively and have frequently structured their teaching around the exemplary behaviour of outstanding Christians, so that lessons about Father Damien, Florence Nightingale, Mother Teresa and others are very frequent. It is right to direct attention to the ethical outcomes of religious adherence and another approach to this is discussed in the article in this section by Clive Erricker on Christian ethics (see pp.75–81).

However, religious behaviour always includes some form of ritual and worship, engaged in by all kinds of adherents, not only the saints and the specially devout. Furthermore, worship is not unrelated to the matter of Christian action. Consider these words of Mother Teresa:

> I cannot do without Mass and Holy Communion. Without Jesus. If I can see Jesus in the appearance of bread then I will be able to see Him in the broken bodies of the poor. That is why I need that oneness with Christ. If I have that deep faith in the Eucharist, naturally I will be able to touch Him in the broken bodies because He has said, I am the Living Bread. (Doig, D. (1976) *Mother Teresa*, London, Collins, p.115)

Worship also implies belief without necessarily articulating it in the form of abstract propositions. So worship is often the most authentic and direct way into the essential nature of Christianity as experienced in the life both of the individual and the community.

THE STYLE OF CHRISTIAN WORSHIP

The distinctive aspect of Christian worship is the distinctive aspect of Christianity itself, namely, Christ. There is of course a long contemplative tradition in Christian worship, but Christian worship is for the most part conceived as *dynamic*. That is, there is felt to be a dialogue, an *encounter*. Because Christians believe that God became man in Christ, it is Christ who is the focus of that encounter between God and man. Human words and actions are lifted into the realm of the spirit where such an exchange takes place.

Christian practice takes account of man's physical nature. Human beings can only express themselves in a physical, spatial manner. In Christ the heavenly, spiritual realm and the earthly, material realm meet. In him the physical is raised up to the spiritual so worship becomes more than aspirations directed towards God but the place of meeting, the encounter with God. This is why Christian prayers so often end with the words 'through Jesus Christ our Lord'. In Christian eyes it is Christ who removes all obstacles to communion with God. Indeed, prayer is often addressed directly to Christ himself. No contradiction is seen in this in so far as God is fully identified in him.

Another feature of Christian worship is that it is fundamentally *communal*. Most Christians would agree that Christ's mission was to bring salvation by means of participation in a redeemed community. The very first description of Christian practice in the Acts of the Apostles indicates that meeting *together* and praying *together* were the accepted norms for worship. Indeed, the breaking of bread as the early typical act of worship emphasises the concept of *sharing*. This does not mean that individual and private worship is inappropriate; but that even private prayer is practised by the individual who sees himself as a member of the 'Church', however defined. Private prayer is understood as a part of the spectrum of Christian worship and requires its due place and consideration. However, pupils should be discouraged from thinking that private prayer is the essence of Christian worship or even its most typical manifestation.

THE 'PHENOMENA' OF CHRISTIAN WORSHIP

By 'phenomena' I mean simply 'those things which are seen to happen'. It is useful to classify worship in terms of a specific perspective. Of course, as we have seen, the overriding focus is Christ, but Christ is implicated in different ways. Three typical Christian perspectives are:

(a) the 'Word', i.e. the perspective of the Scriptures;
(b) the Sacraments; and
(c) the Spirit.

I do not intend here to pursue the theological question of the relationship between them, but only to see these as ways of ordering the material. It is also clear that each of these perspectives is given varied emphasis in particular Churches. The Word indicates that more attention will be given to preaching and proclamation, for example in the Reformed Churches. The Sacraments find greater prominence in the Catholic and Orthodox Churches and in particular one finds here more emphasis on and frequent celebration of the Mass (or Lord's Supper or Holy Liturgy). The Spirit has been chosen to represent the kind of worship which displays greater spontaneity – and to some extent unpredictability. This is of course the rudest of classifications and each group would rightly protest that all three perspectives appear in their worship. There are other ways of classifying, of course, such as the degree to which fixed and traditional forms are used.

TEACHING AIMS

Teaching about Christian worship should lead to:
1. an understanding of its distinctiveness. (Namely, it is concerned with the relationship between man and God through Christ);
2. an awareness of the different styles and their perspectives. (This should include a sense of the particular approaches of different traditions.);
3. some penetration of the feelings of a Christian worshipper and the adoption of a sympathetic attitude towards those feelings;
4. some sense of the continuity of the traditions and forms of Christian worship;
5. an awareness and appreciation of the cultural and aesthetic dimension.

TEACHING MODES AND STRATEGIES

The way in which the teacher teaches is something which he or she develops through practice. Extending one's range of modes and strategies or acquiring new ones is quite difficult. It often means taking some risks, temporarily abandoning well-tried methods and well-trodden ways.

In proposing certain approaches here I am not asserting the inadequacy of any others – or even suggesting that mine are new! I am, nevertheless, advocating them because I believe them to be pedagogically sound and at the same time faithful to the phenomena being examined.

Begin with the phenomena

Given the training received by many RE teachers it is not surprising that there is strong presumption in favour of an historical or theological approach. That is to say, in this instance, one would begin with the formation of the early Church in the New Testament and proceed to trace the development of the various forms of worship, or one would begin with the theological matter of the nature of God and the Incarnation and endeavour to relate worship to theological propositions.

This is often not a very engaging way to begin. I favour beginning directly with the phenomenon being studied. Religious Education should be concerned primarily with living religion and it should help pupils to interpret the examples of living religion which they can see. The visible items of Christian worship could be one of the following: a church near the school, a local priest or minister, a lectern Bible, a crucifix, a rosary, an artefact used in the Eucharist, e.g. a chalice and paten, candles, bread, wine, a prayer book and so on. One can make an entry *at any point*. As teachers we need to learn that the logical manner in which we eventually order our knowledge is not necessarily the best way to learn it. Whatever we begin with, we should try to make it visible or even have it to hand! I was on a conducted tour of a cathedral recently when the guide attempted to tell us all about misericordes without actually showing us one. The boredom was almost palpable! We need to remind ourselves that in teaching it is *always* worth the trouble to provide a concrete, visible example.

Engage the pupils

It may seem rather an obvious piece of advice, but how often do we proceed with our 'input' before we are sure that the pupils have 'engaged'? Some things are inherently interesting, others only become interesting as we learn more. At the minimal level, the teacher needs to raise some questions, so that minds begin to be curious about the answers. Sometimes it is a good idea just to invite the pupils to discuss with each other what their feelings are on the topic.

Another alternative might be to ask the pupils to imagine they are in a church and that they have been asked to sit quietly in silent prayer. After a short, but noticeable, period of silence some should be asked to share what they were thinking about. See also Nora Horrigan's 'A long day at the Vatican' on p.94. Some other versions of this method are clearly possible.

From the initial engagement should arise a certain number of directions to be explored.

The way in which these are explored will depend on the specific topic, the resources available and the expertise of the teacher. It will be important at each stage to allow for pupils to respond. It is preferable that they are not always asked to say what *they* think, but sometimes to say what a 'Christian' thinks or feels or to try and explain what he or she means.

TEACHING POINTS IN RELATION TO WORSHIP

1. It is not part of the teacher's job to determine the validity or 'truth' of any particular form of worship. This is something teachers coming from a Christian standpoint more readily accept in relation to worship in non-Christian religions. But they tend to be *parti pris* in the case of their own. We need to remember

that the task is to understand sympathetically what is *in fact* practised.

Of course pupils do not need to be shielded from the fact that there is, and has been, controversy in Christian practice over, for example, questions like the Real Presence, the use of images, the ordination of women, etc. On the contrary, lively discussion of these matters can give an extra impetus to study. However, the above tenet must stand. It is not the teacher's job to determine which view is 'true'. This is not the same as *not having a view.* The teacher does not have to be personally neutral but needs to be procedurally neutral. This simply means that, for the purposes of teaching the topic in hand, the teacher is not seeking to lead the pupils to adopt a particular viewpoint. Indeed, the teacher will be trying very hard to make sure that opposing views are fairly presented. It is quite unrealistic and dishonest for the teacher to pretend that he or she has no view. But this is very far from *pressing* for the acceptance of a particular view.

2. Christianity is such an outwardly diverse phenomenon that teachers need to make sure that there is a reasonable spread across the different traditions. It is furthermore geographically so widespread that it is important to include some means of showing worship in different cultural settings.

Having said so much about diversity, I would want to add that the Christian movement towards unity in worship should also receive some attention. The work of the Ecumenical Movement (the World Council of Churches) in coming to an 'agreed text' for the Eucharist is a remarkable achievement. The special efforts towards worship in the Community at Taizé in France are intrinsically interesting since they involve so many young people.

3. The language of worship should be distinguished from the language of theology. It is much more akin to poetry. Thus, the penetration of the meaning of worship requires an affective sensitivity more than intellectual cognition. It is worthwhile trying to improve your pupils' vocabulary of symbols, both verbal and material. 'The heavens declare the glory of God and the firmanent sheweth his handiwork' is an example of the poetry of praise. But consider also the use of the *aids* – for example, the use of icons in Orthodoxy; the use of the crucifix or cross as a focus of worship; the symbolism of churches in their ground plan and their atmosphere; and the use of music in services and the development of hymns. All this points to the need to include visits and some kind of participation or imaginative reconstruction. It is desirable that all these explorations take place in relation to people, i.e. people *using* the words and artefacts, whether this is by direct encounter or by the use of texts. In a television series some years ago a monk was asked to say what prayer was. He replied that there was no such thing as prayer – only people praying.

4. It is better to keep 'worship', as a concept, separate from other Christian rites and sacraments. The Eucharist is, of course, included in a study of worship, but other rites like baptism, marriage, burial rites are best dealt with as separate topics. Although logically cognate they raise a whole host of issues not strictly related to worship and one can find oneself diverted from the central concern.

5. Although I have suggested keeping other rites separate, the same does not apply to the study of festivals which in themselves could be a useful starting point for the study of worship. The only danger here is to treat the particular celebrations in a specific festival as if they were the norm. The Christian calendar observed

by most Christians can be a fruitful starting-point in the study of worship.

A POSSIBLE TEACHING SEQUENCE OVER A TERM

A visit to a local church
Reflection on pupil reactions
The consideration of the functions of a building
The examination and discussion of some hymns
A visit from a local minister (or other member) showing an important instrument
    of worship such as a chalice and discussing the Eucharist or Lord's Supper
A more structured study of the Eucharist and the consideration of another 'style'
    of celebration (perhaps another visit, e.g. to a Baptist church, or the use of slides)
Imaginative activity (movement, music, poetry)
Worship at Taizé (slide tape sequence available from Mowbrays)
Discussion of reactions
Some outcome such as a 'Book of Christian Worship' produced by the class, an
    oral presentation or individual writing.

CONCLUSION

Studying worship in Christianity is simply one of the ways of following the principle that Religious Education is more profitable when directed in the first instance towards the *practice* of religion rather than its propositions, and in the hands of a good teacher it can bring insights not available through bald credal statements. It also corrects the over-emphasis on the ethics of religion which tends to occur in school, often depriving pupils of a glimpse of the vision and motivation which believers sense at the heart of their faith.

9 Christian festivals

Mary Hayward

Christian festivals impinge on public consciousness, and thus on children's consciousness, perhaps more than any other aspect of Christianity. As September begins, the commercial face of Christmas becomes apparent, and not long after 6 January Easter eggs appear prematurely — anticipating both the seasonal cycle in the northern hemisphere and the liturgical cycle of the Church. Additionally, in Britain, the two great festivals of the Christian Church — Christmas and Easter — are 'markers' in the secular calendar. These factors are not without significance: arguably these festivals bridge the gap between the sacred and secular worlds; and even those with no professed commitment to the Christian faith become caught up in these celebrations. This is in itself worth considering. Though the faith community may comment unfavourably on the secularisation of the festivals, those with no particular faith are perhaps unlikely to have taken a comparable stance towards the festivals' religious manifestations and significance, present residually, but maybe unidentified, in their own experience. This is not to pin a Christian label on those who would not claim it for themselves, but rather to recognise that the tradition carries within itself questions, perceptions and answers relating to the human condition, and that these are voiced within the multiplicity of the experiences which constitute such 'festivals'.

There is a further dimension to note here. Whilst the Judaeo-Christian tradition embraces a linear concept of time, both traditions — Jewish and Christian — utilise a cyclical model in their calendars. In Christianity there is the liturgical cycle, but more particularly, in the west, the seasonal cycle: Easter coincides with spring as its Anglo-Saxon name denotes; Christmas, with its symbolism of light, falls at the darkest time of the year, appropriating the pagan festivities of earlier times. Such appropriation is well known as one way in which Christianity was able to gain ground in alien environments. School texts sometimes speak with amazing alacrity and certainty of this pre-Christian past, drawing attention to surviving but now 'curious' festivities. But beyond the curiosities, and indeed the process of appropriation, the coincidence of Christian festivals and natural cycles directs attention both to the interrelation of man and his environment, and to his dependence upon it as well as his inter-dependence within it. So, beneath the existential questions articulated within the celebration of the festival *per se*, lies this further stratum.

All this is suggestive of a rich resource for Religious Education and, incidentally, of the 'shape' Religious Education may take. A quick survey of Agreed Syllabuses reveals the popularity of festivals as an area for study in the primary and middle years of education: yet festivals, like good stories, have many layers of meaning, some perhaps accessible only long after school has been left behind. To confine their exploration to the early years of education may be to hinder growth in an understanding both of the Christian tradition and of the concept of a 'festival'. Older students are unlikely to encounter festivals as an area of study: the demise of much of what might be termed Religious Education in the core curriculum deprives the majority of such an opportunity, and 'what is on offer' in the Religious Studies examination syllabus determines the path of those who choose the subject. Where festivals form part of examination syllabuses it is salutary to note that students frequently struggle with questions requiring more than the simple recall of information. Of Christian festivals in particular, I found that those of my students who chose to write about these for their examination projects found it most difficult to bring together appropriate material for their studies. There were few accessible resources which went beyond the boundaries of seasonal customs and few students thought to focus on the *celebration of the Christian community* until pointed in that direction and helped to realise its potential for their work!

So far we have hinted at the potential of the study of festivals — and here we mean Christian festivals — in Religious Education and have noted in brief some facets of their current placing and study in school. In what follows, attention will be given to the value of festivals as a means of Religious Education and an attempt will be made to develop a simple model for exploring the world of festivals and for considering their functions within the Christian community.

RELIGIOUS EDUCATION AND FESTIVAL

Acknowledgement of the need for religious education to relate to the interests and concerns of the pupil has been prevalent for many years. In the 'themework' and 'problem-centred RE' which characterised the Religious Education of the late 1960s and early 1970s, the teacher's task, often within the framework of confessional aims, was to make connections between the world of the child and that of religious faith. Such connections were often tenuous and artificial. The intention 'to make connections' is no doubt sound, but how is this to be done without depending on the juxtaposition of different worlds?

An issue which Religious Education does not seem to have faced is *how far a sensitive handling of specifically religious material, in its own right, allows human interests and concerns to come through*, interests and concerns with which the pupil may readily identify. Inherent in much of the material available to Religious Education are basic human concerns – fears, hopes, expectations, questions and affirmations – provided the material is 'allowed to speak'. If we look for materials to test this viewpoint, festivals provide a useful case study. In the first instance we have already noted that in themselves they bridge the sacred and secular worlds and that because of their 'multi-media' and non-cerebral forms of expression they have wide appeal and offer many levels and points of contact to which the individual may respond.

A MODEL FOR EXPLORING CHRISTIAN FESTIVALS

In offering a model a number of caveats are first necessary. In this country the diversity of the Christian tradition is probably more readily recognised than that of other traditions. A discussion among educational representatives from a number of Christian Churches was livelier than usual when the BBC's Radiovision programme *Easter* (1984) was viewed, yet the visual presentation, apart from a seasonal note of new life, was heavily dependent on the Anglican tradition, and indeed on a particular style of Anglicanism. The filmstrip simply did not reflect the diversity of the Christian Church, or even that of Anglicanism. A certain injustice was felt among those present. Yet, paradoxically, there was something to be learnt here: namely, that the liturgical drama of Easter in one Church might be unacceptable to another. This is related here partly as a reminder, both of diversity and of unity – since the two great festivals are shared by all Christians. Moreover, it is told to encourage the use of the model in a thoughtful and sensitive way. Thus, for example, the visual symbol and action of the Easter liturgy in the Orthodox Church may be the verbal symbol of hymn and song in a Methodist church, and indeed part of the structure of the building in a Baptist church!

In the model of a festival which is offered here, four elements are distinguished: story, symbol, the celebrating community, and experience and meaning. In reality, of course, they are interwoven in the keeping of a festival. They are also interrelated with the rest of a school's Religious Education programme. For example, our pupils' understanding of the concept of a story in the context of a festival, and their capacity to grasp its meaning, may depend on the opportunities they have had to grapple with this form of expression elsewhere in RE – or indeed in English literature.

Story

Story has recently come to the fore in Religious Education, and for many – twenty years on from Ronald Goldman's research – this has begun to make biblical material once more 'respectable'. But of course the rediscovery of story is not so simple. It isn't just an open invitation to tell stories and to consider 'that's RE covered', not even if the teacher selects those which she thinks children can understand, or which are deemed a part of their cultural heritage, or even those which offer the opportunity to put across a moral point in assembly! Story in world faiths does have a context: a context in a believing community, and frequently within its worship and its festivals. This is particularly true of the Christian tradition; here story is both the creation of the community and creative of that community.

An exploration of the dimensions of story within a religious tradition may not be undertaken here, but three facets can be highlighted. They relate to the way in which stories function. The first facet is located on the *individual level* where they have the capacity to involve the whole person, and where they invite personal engagement. Through the vehicle of story-telling new perspectives may be opened up, with all their potential for change and growth. The point was clearly made in the 'story issue' of the *British Journal of Religious Education*:

> We willingly suspend our disbelief for the purposes of enjoying a fantasy journey and allow ourselves to be carried through strange territory. But we do not return to the former ground of our existence the same persons who temporarily left it. In some way which evades close description, our mental outlook and emotional repertoire have altered or evolved.
> (Sullivan, J. (1982) 'Stories of commitment', *British Journal of Religious Education*, 4 (3), pp.129)

Arguably there is something of this process afoot as crowds are 'drawn' annually to hear again 'the story' of Christmas.

A second facet refers to the fact that the stories which are told in a religious context articulate *what the community believes to be of ultimate importance*. Each story is thus bound up with identity: it marks out boundaries; it is a unifying force. But stories also possess a latent power as we noted earlier, and so they may become also a source of creative tension within a community as successive generations come to terms with their meanings.

A third facet derives from the fact that the telling of the story *within the context of an annual cycle of festivals offers continuity within the tradition.* Each festival, through a richness of symbol and celebration, 'makes present' the events which it recalls; responses are evoked, and reaffirmation and renewal mark out a continuing path and quest.

Where a story and a festival combine, these three facets — the individual and communal responses, and the continuity of tradition — cohere; they are true of both festival and story. They also suggest directions for teaching. For example, hearing the story, the time to reflect, the time to consider responses (across cultures and generations, 'in' and 'out' of the believing community — not forgetting of course that the stories as they have been preserved are themselves responses) and, indeed, the time to respond, all become part of the learning process.

I suspect that many teachers already engage children in just this kind of process; but consider a class of 11–12 year olds during their first term in secondary school. Each member of the class was asked to bring a 'religious' Christmas card to the lesson. A simple task was set: which story does your card tell? Matthew's? Luke's?

Both? And another task: does your card seem to 'add' any information to the stories you've discovered? Imagine some responses:

This card has snow — *would* there have been snow, Miss?

They don't look as though they're in a stable here — it looks more like a palace to me.

My card seems to have most of the story missing — it's just a large star and a tiny building in the distance.

The mother and baby look Chinese on John's card: that can't be right!

Ah! Look at Debbie's card, Miss — it's got rabbits and robins and Mary and Joseph and the shepherds look really cute.

A simple approach! What has been achieved? Firstly, engagement with the Christmas *stories*. And having identified their distinctness, 'Why are there two?' This becomes a real question to follow up at a later date, offering the opportunity to penetrate beyond the detail to purpose and meaning — and theologies! The idea of information 'being added' opens up many possibilities: the snow — an echo of pre-Christian times, or the acculturation of the festival?; stable or palace — an entry into the paradox and mystery of the Christmas stories; the star — recognition of the language of sign and symbol, the poetic quality of the narratives; the Chinese virgin and child — the universality of story and response; the 'cute' card — the making marginal and neutralisation of the story? Throughout, the children are encountering 'the story' and responses to it. The task provides a vehicle too for their own responses.

Symbol

The issue of symbolisation is not unrelated to story-telling. Christian stories raise the issue of truth in an acute sense for the teacher, and for the pupil. 'Is the story true?' If the question is voiced by children, it means 'Did events happen in this way?' But alongside this the question 'Is the story true?' must remain, not as an empirical issue, but as one which has both theological and existential dimensions. For a moment we will sidestep the question as it applies to the Christian context and consider a story from the Hindu tradition.

Children in my lower secondary school happily engaged with the now widely known festival of Diwali and with the story of the return of Rama and Sita from exile which distinguishes its celebration in some parts of India. The story the Ramayana tells did not 'trouble' the children in the empirical sense noted earlier. Asked 'Why do you think the story has been remembered?' children responded with a range of answers: the part played by animals will always be enjoyed by children; there are many loyalties in the story — Sita to Rama, Lakshmana to Rama, Bharata to Rama; Sita is a good and perfect wife; animals and humans co-operate; but above all good triumphs — or, if I may put it in Hindu terms, dharma is restored. Such responses pick up both insights into Hindu tradition, and the existential concerns of the story, and they move in the direction of replying 'Yes' to the question 'Is it true?'

So what of Christian story? How do we cope with an angel appearing to a young woman; with dreams; with an apparent flaunting of accepted morality; with wise men following a star; with shepherds hearing heavenly choirs — to take examples from the Christmas stories? One problem is that on the surface the stories appear to read as narrative, and are widely read as historical narrative. Here Luke 2:1–2 is worth some reflection. Is the evangelist really interested in establishing a date, at this point or elsewhere, or is he making a statement about Jesus — and which is the more important? The situation is compounded by the fact that Christians themselves do not agree about how these stories should be read. But beyond all this, if questions are asked about their continuing 'appeal' — even among those whose links with the Christian community may be tenuous — it is to the stories' affirmation about 'how things really are', to the commentary they offer on human experience and to the theology they contain that we must look.

If we ask 'Is it true?' in the sense in which we asked this of the Ramayana, what might be highlighted? The stories tell of promises being kept (fulfilled); of a new order of priorities prevailing among mankind and the transformation of society; of the dignity of all and not just the rich; of a birth and all its potential; of a meeting of the worlds of God and men, which makes all these things possible; of paradox and mystery — the child who is helpless but King; of peace and hope and of much more. Perhaps it should be admitted that the stories may not so easily reveal their insights as those which we considered from the Ramayana. The Christmas stories are already interpreted and they reveal more layers of meaning as they are examined in the light of a Christian reading of Jewish scripture (as indeed do those associated with Easter and Pentecost), and as they are approached from the perspective of the earliest Christian communities reflecting on their experience of Jesus. To indicate these perspectives is to mark out an agenda for the upper school and sixth form studies. But at all levels, the appropriate approach is to see these stories as more akin to poetry than to 'fact'; and to allow them to function symbolically, exploring what they point to — but without destroying their 'wholeness'.

This kind of exploration may also be helped by the use of visual material. Children I taught in the first year at secondary school spent some time considering a large print of Gentile da Fabriano's *Adoration of the Magi,*[1] painted in Florence *c.* 1423 and now in the Uffizi Gallery. The picture is full of detail and movement, and seems to appeal to that age group. The paradox I refer to above is delightfully present. The child is at once child-like — withdrawing a toe as it catches on a wise man's beard — but also stretching out a hand in blessing over the wise man's head, as he, dressed in resplendent kingly robes, stoops low at the foot of the child. This is not the reversal of fortunes of the 'mighty laid low' but a visual symbol nonetheless of a new order. The cavalcade of those who come to see the child also speaks; here is journeying and questing. And who is this birth for? Many are in rich Florentine merchant costume, but what of the man removing a wise man's spurs in the foreground — is he servant or thief?

At a much more pragmatic level consider the social concern of the Christmas season. What about collections and appeals from charities — from Christian and non-Christian organisations? Why especially are such requests made at Christmas? Does this question lead back to 'the story'? Is the story 'at work' here?

I have been suggesting that the stories associated with festivals may function symbolically — and that, in RE, ways of discovering this function need to be explored. Many of the 'tangible' symbols of Christmas, however, are not derived from the Christmas stories. For example, holly and other evergreens, the Christmas tree (replacing the oak) and feasting belong to a pre-Christian past. They take us back to the cyclical view of existence which we noted at the beginning of this chapter: the natural cycle, the dependence of man on nature. In these symbols we can begin to see how Christianity appropriated older customs, that is, assimilated them and gave them a Christian meaning. The prevalence and potency of such symbols necessitated their continuation, but on Christian terms. Many carols reflect this duality. A glance at Puritan history will reveal a suspicion of such festivities: the balance of 'pagan' and 'Christian' was a delicate one – perhaps it is matched by the secular–Christian balance of festivals in the present. How the two interrelate might be a theme for older students to explore.

The celebrating community

Celebration implies community and Christian community characteristically implies worship. In the context of worship, Christmas and Easter – the latter culminating in Pentecost – make a profound mark on the calendar. Both involve periods of preparation, and of anticipation, which add to the solemnity of the festival and help to distinguish its religious from its secular celebration. Such periods may also place the festivals in the wider setting of 'salvation-history'. Of course, as we have noted earlier, not all Christians celebrate in the same way, but their worship provides a context in which the key moments of a shared story, already marked out by annual festivals, may have 'immediacy'. Such immediacy may be communicated in many ways, but it is nevertheless this quality which invites response and thus brings renewal and continuity for the community.

For Religious Education this poses the question of how children may meet the celebrating community defined in this way. The issue is further confused by the schools' own celebration of the Christmas festival – even if Easter is neglected – and indeed by the wider question of the statutory requirement of worship in schools which are secular institutions. The latter point cannot be pursued here; with regard to the former, Religious Education departments will frequently find themselves involved with school celebrations which take on 'religious' overtones (and which may for some constitute worship). Can the RE department draw a distinction between the school's celebration and that within the faith community? I believe it must; its proper concern is with understanding the latter, its contribution to the former may *then* be to help others in the school community to *understand* the Christian dimensions of a festival. It is interesting that T. Shannon's *Christmas and Easter* (Cambridge, Lutterworth Press, 1984) includes a chapter entitled 'Your Easter Liturgy'. Here, students who have studied the drama of the Orthodox Easter Liturgy are helped to plan their own, and thus to apply what they have understood. Perhaps this kind of activity can bridge the gap which may so easily exist between what is understood and enjoyed in RE and what is experienced in assembly, allowing students to share what they have discovered.

For this to happen successfully much is asked of RE! So how may children encounter the celebrating community and its worship? This seems to be an area to which few books on festivals give much attention. Trevor Shannon's is an exception. The comment of one examination student offers a starting point: 'Most churches are old, very draughty, and cold, yet every time I visit one, especially on festive occasions, I feel warm inside.' So, consider Easter. It may be visibly experienced in a church building (the problems of visits to 'empty' buildings should not lead the RE teacher to reject them too readily) and explored through slides[2] if visits are not possible. Look at the plainness of many churches during Lent; the absence of colour and the additional solemnity of Passion Sunday. Contrast the temporary 'lightening' of mood on Palm Sunday and the decorations of palm and willow, with the ominous red furnishings of the day, the stripped church of Maundy Thursday and Good Friday, and then the transformation of colour and light on Easter Day. Something of mood and feeling and of a community remembering can be conveyed in this way. It may be supplemented by an exploration of the liturgical drama of Holy Week, perhaps met through slides,[3] or video,[4] or personal contacts.[5] The Taizé community in France[6] has made of each weekend a 'mini-Easter' built around the symbolism of darkness and light, death and life, derived from the Easter vigil. Coventry Cathedral, which in its structure speaks of death and resurrection, conveys also a message of reconciliation: its litany of reconciliation[7] prayed every Friday at twelve noon by the charred cross in the ruins, adds another dimension to the pupils' understanding of worship and − like the Taizé material − helps them to grasp something of the pervasive nature of festival. Though highlighted at specific moments, its message is carried into the rest of the year, in the community and in individual lives. Perhaps this is suggestive of another entry into festival − the ways in which its meaning is embraced by individuals. I remember many years ago an effective Easter programme for schools which told the story of Dr Mary Verghese. I have heard one teacher relate how she drew on Sheila Cassidy's experience,[8] exploring the mystery of suffering which is part of the Easter experience of the Christian community.

Experience and meaning

Story, symbol and celebration have already taken us into the realm of meaning and experience, it could not be otherwise, and I always feel some impatience with books about festivals for pupils which explore these facets of festival and then add 'meaning' at the end. Somehow they have 'missed the point' of festival.[9] My argument here has been that story, symbol and celebration *convey meaning and 'match' human experience* (and that means the children's too!) as they interact and as the Christian, or even the casual observer, becomes caught up in their dynamic. As Trevor Shannon's book *Christmas and Easter* concludes:

The Christian festivals... bring before Christians the great questions of life and death... By celebrating the festivals a Christian becomes involved in the events and the meaning of the life of Jesus − his birth, his death and his resurrection. In this way a Christian is helped to face the questions in his own life, and to share the joy of the Christian good news — that life is transformed by love, and out of death comes life.

The task of Religious Education is to let festivals 'speak'.

NOTES

1. The picture may be found in Kossoff, D. (1977) *The Christmas Story*, London, Collins & World.

2. and 3. The Slide Centre Ltd, Ilton, Ilminster, Somerset, TA19 9HS, produces the following slides which are helpful here:
S1464   *Christian Churches: the Significant Features*
S1473   *Holy Week — Palm Sunday and Maundy Thursday*
S1474   *Holy Week — Good Friday*
S1475   *Holy Week — Holy Saturday and Easter Day*
Readers may also find the BBC Radiovision filmstrip *Easter* (1984) helpful.

4. ITV's *Believe It or Not* series includes a programme on the Orthodox tradition (Serbian) which focuses on the celebration of Easter. *Aspects of Christianity* from Videotext Educational Publishing and Exmouth School, Department of Religion, includes an 'Orthodox Easter Night Procession'.

5. Personal experience may also come through written pieces; see, for example, Shannon, T. (1984) *Christmas and Easter*, Cambridge, Lutterworth Press, p.18 (chapter entitled 'The Christmas Eucharist').

6. See, for example, *Taizé: That Little Springtime* a video distributed in this country by A.R. Mowbray Ltd, who also have available a slide-tape sequence about Taizé.

7. Copies of this litany are available from Coventry Cathedral bookshop.

8. See Cassidy, S. (1977) 'Prayer under duress' in *The Light of Experience*, BBC.

9. This is an unfortunate feature of *Christmas* and *Easter* in RMEP's popular Living Festivals series.

10 Christian communities

Alan Brown

The central feature of the Christian religion is that of community. This is a contentious statement, for many Christians would argue, with some vigour, that the central figure or feature of their religion was Jesus; or indeed that the Bible, too, was more central than the concept of community. Yet for people not acquainted with Christianity what they see is people coming together in various groups for various reasons; in other words, Christians appear to gather together in diverse communities to celebrate and share their faith with each other. However, it is not only this 'objective' view that underlines the importance of the community, for most Christians would acknowledge that they belong to 'the Church', if this term is used in its broadest sense, and that they are part of the 'body of Christ' (though not all Christians would use that term). Christians are bound together in community through the theological axioms of their faith, so the student of Christianity can only begin to understand Christian religious experience if serious account is taken of this need for Christians to come together for worship.

The teacher has to point the pupil in the direction of what Christian communities are, how they may be defined and what their basic characteristics are. Some signposts are needed which will help pupil understanding of why Christians gather together and how they find a sense of meaning and purpose within a community. It would be extremely difficult to produce a definition of what is a Christian community unless one could spend a considerable time looking at a wide variety of such communities. The range of communities chosen for study in the classroom makes such a definition impossible and undesirable.

There is one basic assumption made in this article, namely, that Christianity, in all its many forms, is paradoxically concerned with the fulfilment of the individual − the achievement of the full potential of each person − yet this aim can only be carried out if that person is identified as a part of the community of the body of Christ. This assumption may not be acceptable to all, but it seems, at least, a defensible statement of what it means to be a Christian. The Christian could claim that personal salvation is made possible through the saving act of God in Jesus and that this personal salvation is merely celebrated in, or through, a community. Christianity is not alone in being a religion built on paradox but unless this dichotomy is recognised and reconciled one cannot really begin to understand how Christian communities operate.

Each Christian community has to speak for itself and the whole corporate body of the 'Church' is paradoxically more than the sum total of its individual communities. The search to bring home to the pupil the complexity of community life is never-ending but the themes touched on in the Chichester Project include:

(a)   the individual is fulfilled within a community;
(b)   the essential nature of a community as part of the 'body of Christ';
(c)   the diversity of communities and communal life;
(d)   the necessity of some form of discipline or self-discipline;
(e)   the importance of the strength of personalities in any community;
(f)   the lack of unanimity and uniformity within a community;
(g)   the provisional nature of some communities compared to the historical tradition of others.

The sub-titles reflect this contrasting quality of Christian community, but this is a creative tension in which opposites do not oppose but add to a greater understanding of the nature of community.

PERMANENT OR PROVISIONAL

This notion of paradox is exemplified through a study of the community at Taizé, for that community challenges a number of stereotypes that cling to a monastic community. It is interesting not only because of its commitment to young people but also because its founder is a Protestant. For many pupils it appears that all monks are Roman Catholic and have something to do with St Francis, etc., so to examine an order of monks founded fairly recently by a Protestant seems appropriate. Furthermore, the Taizé community is ecumenical, its monks coming from the Roman Catholic, Protestant and Anglican Churches. The theme of individuality is retained and developed within the community, for even though the monks have taken the traditional vows of poverty, chastity and obedience to the Prior, Roger, they still retain their individual allegiance to the Church of their choice. It may seem that this is too subtle for many children to grasp but, conceptually, it is not very different from the notion that boys and girls from different religions and countries can be members of the Scout and Guide movement. There has to be general agreement about certain basic principles but within these bounds the individuality of each person is recognised and respected. Of course, it must be said, at Taizé this divergence is used as a means of highlighting the scandal of division within the Christian Church as a whole, which is focused most clearly in the celebration of the Eucharist where Roman Catholics receive the sacrament separately from the rest.

Religious communities can appear permanent: they may have been in existence for centuries and inhabit imposing buildings that have been built to last. But Taizé is provisional. The Taizé community deliberately tries not to create its own history — it lives for the present and the future. Records are destroyed each year and the community effectively lives with its bags packed. This is an often neglected aspect of many Christian communities. Some communities value and savour centuries of tradition but Taizé, like some others, tries to capture the immediacy and provisional nature of Christian response. Perhaps people come closest to this when they take photographs, keep mementoes (a bus ticket, pebble, etc.), then one day have a clear out and such things are all thrown away. The past is important but only because it contributes to the making of the present and we must grow away from clinging memories of past years.

UNITY AND INDIVIDUALISM

The Iona community is an example of the corporate individuality of many communities. In this case the island of Iona became a symbol of renewal, through its historical traditions connected with Columba — a renewal of the importance of work, of hope to the unemployed, as well as a spiritual renewal for some Christians. This community is not one of monks, it is a mixture of clergy and laity, men and women, who retain their Christian individuality as members of a number of different Churches, but who commit themselves to each other in prayer, in spiritual and material ways, that are focused on the symbol of Iona. The fact that they rarely all meet together, though many meet once or twice a year, shows how a community may be one even though its members are scattered.

These principles show how a community like Iona can represent a useful contrast to Taizé, for while the latter is provisional and just happens to be based at Taizé by historical accident, Iona has an historical and a religious tradition stretching back even beyond Columba's settlement. Within the Iona community one is an individual making a personal commitment to a largely unseen community — nonetheless one is a member of that group. The island has become a symbol of Christianity and has known many types of Christian community. These have changed their nature and have ebbed and flowed over the centuries. Now it is largely a symbol of the Community's commitment to working in the world — in ordinary jobs — rebuilding people's lives in the same way that George McLeod rebuilt the Abbey. This is a crucial element in the study of any Christian community: the way in which it establishes itself in relation to the person of Jesus and to the immediate society in which it finds itself.

DISCIPLINE AND FREEDOM

Whilst the two communities referred to above contrast in certain ways, they still retain some important similarities, so a further dimension can only be established through looking at a teaching order, teaching being a traditional activity of monks and nuns. The nuns of the Order of the Holy Paraclete take the traditional vows of poverty, chastity and obedience, live in a local community, but have a worldwide concern and impact as do the monks of Taizé. Like the Iona community, they were established in a town with a long (Christian) history, where St Hilda's spiritual presence complemented that of St Columba. The similarities extend further in that each community was committed to activities which took them out into the world, inspired by founders who possessed strong charismatic personalities.

The point is that while each community may have a distinctive quality there must be points of overlap because of their very natures as Christian communities. This means, of course, that each member must have a commitment not only to the truth of the Christian message but to other members of the community. This involves discipline and self-discipline, so it seems appropriate to remind oneself that all communities require a strong sense of discipline and self-discipline and the Order of the Holy Paraclete has a rigorous discipline *as well as* a teaching responsibility.

Many pupils and some teachers have little experience of religious communities so it is important to give a brief glimpse of life at a school run by nuns. Of course rules and discipline change but if one can appreciate how a boarding school with a strong religious presence is run, then it is easier to recognise how a comprehensive school is run on quite different lines. Schools are communities but a religious school provides a further dimension to the meaning of the concept of community. Here pupils and nuns overlap with each other, the religious community providing a base for members of another sort of community. This represents a key feature of Christian communities; they overlap rather like mathematical sets so each person can be a member of several communities at once, yet each one represents a different feature of the individual's Christianity. Individuality is, if you like, built up by the communality experienced by that individual in different Christian (and other) communities. All the communities contribute to this but the Order of the Holy Paraclete is a good example of a community largely living together in one place but providing an educational service for the world 'out there'.

STABILITY AND GROWTH

Pupils often appear to believe that the edifice of the Church appeared fully formed. Therefore the aims of any teaching about early Christian communities must be to reaffirm the importance of the individual within the community; establish the provisional quality of life felt by the early Christians; indicate the strength of personalities present in the early Church; and break up the monolithic view often held by people about the early Church. One might approach this by underlining the differences of opinion that existed between Peter and Paul. The Church had not yet sorted itself out and through these differences it is possible to show that the community could not have been forged as a unity at that time. One of the important features of the early Christian community was its strength of belief, though this belief was tied to an uncertainty of how best it could be expressed, and how to create a community in which a sense of unity could be established. Seeds were being sown for the differentiation of later Christianity. Paul provides a good example of how the centre of Christianity began to move from its Jewish background in Israel to the Graeco-Roman culture of Rome. Who knows, perhaps the seeds of the schism between the Roman and the Orthodox Churches were sown in these early years?

One can never really divorce content from teaching method and it is important to enable the pupil to experiment in a role-playing situation. Without fear of committing themselves they are able to explore some of the problems of living in a community and having to come to terms with other people's different beliefs, practices and habits. Such activity cannot be a waste of time because one of the ways in which we learn to live in a community is by living in it — it takes time to make friends, know who to ask, where to go, etc. It helps to develop the concept of what a community is and how it develops. All communities are fundamentally concerned with participation; all people are part of one community or another, and role play provides an opportunity where one can 'objectify' one's feelings and opinions. Different groups can each take on a different dynamic, enabling the pupils to learn far more about communities than they are able to do by simply reading a text. Beliefs are not monolithic, they emerge in relation to one's society and the early Church had to come to terms with the widely differing views of what it meant to be a Christian. Do you compromise or not? Whatever your answer, it will have a direct effect on how you live and how you relate to other people!

MINISTER AND MINISTRY

One community which embraces all people is that of the parish, regardless of whether one attends church or believes. This is another aspect of a Christian community, for how can one take responsibility for people who do not share one's beliefs?

What does a minister or vicar do? Well, he does a variety of things but the country is divided into parishes and it is useful for pupils to recognise the diversity within each parish. So, for example, one Anglican parish may well overlap with a Roman Catholic parish, a Methodist church area, a Salvation Army Citadel, etc. Each overlaps the others and is (usually) related to the others in some way.

Another feature the teacher might be able to draw out is how a vicar is the leader or organiser of a community while at the same time being the person who ministers to, or serves, that same community. One could argue that all Christian leaders, whether they belong to a hierarchical Church or not, are both leaders and servants of their communities. This is a difficult concept to grasp, particularly for pupils whose schools will, in the main, reflect a hierarchical structure and it will not always be clear to them that, for example, the headteacher is the 'leader' of the school yet is also 'ministering' to their needs.

Finally, it is so common to hear that clergy 'only work on Sundays' that it is useful to look at two weeks of a clergyman's life. Pupils may choose to compare their lives, of which large areas are ordered for them by the school, with the vicar who has to organise his own life around the widely differing needs of his parishioners. Indeed, this could pick up the themes mentioned earlier of discipline and self-discipline, the individual in the community, etc.

One of the keys to teaching about Christian communities is to engage the pupils in their diversity as individuals and as members of organisations. They develop through meeting a wide variety of people in different contexts, through school, clubs, hobbies, religious groups, etc. When they join a group they make some commitment to it though they still retain their own individuality. So it is with Christian communities − which combine individuality with group unity, stability with growth, and are permanent yet provisional.

11 Christian ethics

Clive Erricker

AT SEA OR ON THE ROAD TO JUDGEMENT?

In John Bunyan's *Pilgrim's Progress* we are introduced to a detailed examination of the Christian life as a road to be travelled, with all its accompanying pitfalls, temptations and snares. Only his resolve and purposeful defiance along with the observance of strict codes of conduct will enable the hero, Christian, to arrive at the prized Celestial City. Here is a good example of just how fundamental right conduct is to the expression of Christianity. As an analogy on which to base a world view it is not the only one appropriate to Christianity. It is also true that the same basic model, that of road and journey, can be and has been used for non-Christian world views, although similar conduct in following the route would not necessarily be advocated, of course. However, this particular mental image does impart its own framework to our thinking and encourage us to think within the bounds of a received model. In other words, it has unconsciously shaped our thinking. It is this idea of shaping I wish to explore within the context of Christian ethics. I think it will prove useful in not only making the complexities of Christian ethical views clearer but in showing how they form a matrix with the analysis of ethics generally.

To illustrate further, consider an alternative model to that of the road. Arthur Koestler, speaking in the general context of how one establishes direction, purpose and correct conduct in one's life, compared the human condition to that of being the captain of a ship setting out with a sealed order in his pocket. He makes two points: the first, that this particular captain's awareness of having orders makes him different to the captain of a pleasure cruiser or pirate ship; and the second, that, having opened his envelope, once at sea, he nevertheless finds the orders to be invisible.

Again, this model can be examined within the context of Christianity or outside it, but for the purposes of this essay I wish to contrast the two models as ways of examining the starting points of different *Christian* ethical positions.

In the 1960s what was termed situation ethics had an enlivening effect on Christian ethical thinking. It was essentially Protestant in character, emphasising the sovereignty of individual decision-making. It was popularised by Joseph Fletcher in the USA and Bishop John Robinson in Britain. It flourished within the context of demythologising in the theological world and permissiveness in western society in general. Situation ethics emphasised Koestler's model of our human condition against Bunyan's by suggesting that Christians cannot arrive at decisions about what is right or wrong by observing unchanging God-given laws about conduct. Rather, Jesus taught that love (*agape*) is the attitude that a Christian should bring to all his moral decision-making and that there are no God-given orders that can be followed to the letter to ensure one does right and not wrong. The situations in which we make moral decisions are not like that; they are too complex. But also what each decision really demands is not a certain set of acts to be avoided but a desire to achieve the right end, the best possible outcome for others. Bunyan's attitude as to what is virtuous and what is to be avoided is alien to the situationist. Koestler's model presents the Christian condition more realistically.

LOVE AND LAW: A PROTESTANT DILEMMA

The debate between law and love is not a uniquely Christian concern or a specifically religious one. As a consequence, I am not suggesting it is a purely Protestant debate within Christianity, but it has been highlighted within the Protestant tradition and it provides a framework for the central issue of how one ensures right conduct. Many of Christianity's critics are reductionist in their approach to Christian morality because they perceive it as being based on the Ten Commandments with the accent on 'Thou shalt not' and the implication that man has no say in what constitutes right or wrong but is expected to adhere unquestioningly to an external moral code of absolutes. This raises two issues. Are the Ten Commandments the foundation of Christian morality? Do the Ten Commandments stand over against man as a set of laws that act solely as a means of judgement on an individual's goodness? As in all religious matters, there is a dangerous tendency to interpret things literally and critics are often as guilty of this failing as are adherents. I have found that classroom discussion has a particular tendency to take on this character and do no more than reinforce antagonisms. One of our aims as teachers should be to lift the pupils' awareness above this. Examining the Ten Commandments is a part of the study of Christian ethics in the same way as looking at codes of action is a part of the study of ethics generally. We should not forget, however, that Jesus summarised the Commandments, enjoining Christians and Jews to love God and love their neighbour as themselves, and that, according to Jesus' teaching, the whole law is based on this. This is not prescriptive of acts but describes a state of being underlying right conduct: 'loving'. Also the Commandments themselves can be interpreted in different ways. See, for example, Erich Fromm's commentary on what it means to keep the Sabbath holy and a day of rest:

Is the Shabbat nothing but a day of rest in the mundane sense of freeing people, at least on one day, from the burden of work? To be sure it is that, and this function gives it the dignity of one of the great innovations in human evolution. Yet if this were all that it was, the Shabbat would hardly have played the central role I have just described. In order to understand this role we must penetrate to the core of the Shabbat institution. It is not rest *per se*, in the sense of not making an effort, physically or mentally. It is rest in the sense of the re-establishment of complete harmony between human beings and between them and nature. Nothing must be destroyed and nothing be built: the Shabbat is a day of truce in the human battle with the world. Even tearing up a blade of grass is looked upon as a breach of this harmony, as is lighting a match. Neither must social change occur. It is for this reason that carrying anything on the street is forbidden, (even if it weighs as little as a handkerchief), while carrying a heavy load in one's garden is permitted. The point is not that the effort of carrying a load is forbidden, but the transfer of any object from one privately owned piece of land to another, because such transfer constituted, originally, a transfer of property. On the Shabbat one lives as if one has nothing, pursuing no aim except being, that is expressing one's essential powers: praying, studying, eating, drinking, singing, making love.

E. Fromm, *To Have or To Be,* (London, Sphere Books, 1979) p57.

So already we should be aware that the situation is more complex than a simple affirmative answer to the above questions would imply.

But Christian ethics takes seriously the causal connection scrutinised in ethics generally, namely that every act has a prior motive(s) and a consequence(s) and how you judge the goodness and badness of a person's behaviour depends on which particular aspect of this process you invest with the most moral significance. This is where the law versus love debate starts.

The following story by P.C. Schumacher illustrates this and is a good entry into the whole problem for older secondary pupils.

A girl is on her way to marry her fiancé. In order to do so she must cross an unswimmable river and a labyrinthine forest for which she must have a guide. To cross the river she asks the boatman to take her across. He replies that he will do so if she will make love to him. Distressed at this, and unable to decide what to do, she goes to a wise man for advice. The wise man simply tells her, 'I cannot help you.' Upon further reflection she agrees to the boatman's offer and he takes her across. She then comes to the forest. The guide is the devil. He agrees to take her through on the same terms as stipulated by the boatman. Having agreed to the boatman she sees no point in sacrificing her aim now and does as the devil decrees. After passing through the forest she meets her fiancé and feels she must tell him of what has happened. On hearing about what she has done he refuses to marry her.

As an exercise, the characters in the story can be ranked in order of moral acceptability. With children the order can vary substantially, though they are often initially unclear as to why. For example, many rank the girl top because it was she who made the greatest effort and sacrificed herself because of her love for her fiancé. Others rank the fiancé top because he stood by his moral principle that sex outside marriage is wrong. The wise man is sometimes ranked top because his was the moral virtue of blamelessness and he told the truth. The boatman tends to appeal to those with a sense of moral anarchy who believe that we are all fundamentally self-seeking and the boatman is not afraid to let this be known (and anyway, it was a form of contract, wasn't it?). As for the devil, well he *is* the devil so it was about 'par for the course' as far as he's concerned, wasn't it? The structure of moral decision-making and how a group have arrived at their judgements can be explored from these initial statements.

Another question can also be asked so that the situation is considered within a Christian context. Which of the characters in the story acted in a Christian way? The devil? Of course not. The boatman? Most unacceptable. The wise man? Yes, possibly. The girl? Often she comes out quite badly here. The fiancé? By contrast, he often comes out well. In other words the 'Who is a Christian?' question highlights some interesting preconceptions, uncertainties and narrownesses as to what can be considered a Christian response and this centres on the decision and actions of the girl and her fiancé.

If we put this into a theological context the girl exemplifies the situationist approach to Christian ethics and the boy is the legalist. Now the aim, at this stage, is not to judge the two positions but to understand them. If we follow our emotions we may already be judging the fiancé as too cold and as lacking in compassion, whilst siding with the girl. If we stand with the fiancé, he is principled and self-sacrificial whilst the girl has no sense of honour, self-respect or purity. Christian quotations can be used to support either side. But our task is *to be aware* that this is what we tend to do, and reflect on that mental process, interrupting it with a suspension of judgement that asks, first of all, what is understandable about the fiancé's response and what is understandable about the girl's. By trying to empathise with the other person's judgement we create dialogue and the possibility of respect, if not agreement. Most importantly, too, the initial threat to one's own judgement posed by another's disagreement is allayed. Within the classroom this hopefully encourages a greater self-confidence and lessens dogmatism. The particular examples provided by authors like Fletcher, in *Situation Ethics*, and Barclay, in *Ethics in a Permissive Society*, can then be discussed and developed as further examples are offered by individuals in the class.

The original story can be elaborated by the substitution of different responses, e.g. the girl kills the boatman or she steals his boat. Are these variations more or less acceptable? Do judgements as to her moral behaviour change? This raises the question of how far we are prepared to justify the achievement of an end by the use of any means and the whole question of the relationship between the two. It also has the advantage of removing the sexual bias of the story and giving it a more general applicability.

What becomes clear, time and again, is that a Christian view of right and wrong is thought to be based primarily, if not solely, on the Ten Commandments and it consists of a number of things being forbidden. The curiousness of this is most apparent when we return to the First Commandment, 'To love the Lord God with all your heart, mind and strength, and your neighbour as yourself.' Here there is no prohibition and no possible legal basis for its enforcement. Why does the misconception remain? I suggest it has something to do with a dualistic view of man in the Christian tradition that also operates within secular society. This is the belief that man is either potentially good, given the opportunity, or potentially bad, if the necessary restrictions are removed. The question of which, the benign or the corrupt nature, is emphasised, and leads to the corresponding emphasis on love or law in our view of morality. Perhaps it is our fear as parents or teachers of a child's wrong-doing that leads to the latter being a so much more familiar view of morality expressed by pupils and students in the classroom.

AUTHORITY AND CONSCIENCE:
A ROMAN CATHOLIC DILEMMA

For Catholicism one of the major contemporary ethical issues has been that of the Church's authority in relation to the individual believer's conscience. For many children this is a difficult experience to imagine in religious terms. Institutionally, their closest parallel is their own conscience as an authority in relation to school rules or paternal discipline. But it is often difficult for them to grasp the notion of the belief in tradition that exists in Catholic countries and communities and the sense of rightness that accompanies obedience to an acknowledged and trusted system of ecclesiastical authority, viz. the sense that it brings of divine guidance in the chaotic world of everyday decision-making. Add to this the difference in cultural upbringing between western societies and many Third World Catholic communities where the Roman Catholic Church has a central social and civic role to play, and the gap is a difficult one to bridge.

It is in this situation that case study and role play are often the most useful strategies. As the bishop of a diocese or the priest of a Christian community, an individual bears the tension of knowing that as he is an official representative of the beliefs he serves, in speaking out against authority, as represented by the ecclesiastical hierarchy as a whole, he undermines that sense of a divinely-guided order that it is the Church's responsibility to bring. He creates a crisis for himself, which may have catastrophic spiritual, psychological and physical consequences for others. This is what the burden of authority entails. Two individual cases that illustrate this are those of Oscar Romero in El Salvador and Camillo Torres in Columbia. A Roman Catholic peasant population with a high level of illiteracy and little comprehension of the distinctive characteristics of political life can be bewildered and destroyed by the ways in which this dilemma is or is not dealt with.

The Pope himself provides a study of even greater complexity. When the Papal encyclical 'Humanae Vitae' was issued by Paul VI on 20 July 1968 there was a great deal of agonised response and significant criticism from both concerned lay people and the priesthood. In his collection of letters and papers responding to the encyclical, *The Pope, the Pill and the People*, Norman St John Stevas writes that, 'Behind the birth control issue lie deeper problems of authority in the Church. Is the Pope's status as absolute ruler tolerable for Catholics in the modern world?' Of course, the answer to this last question is for Catholics to decide. Within the parameters of a study of ethics in teaching Christianity we simply want to understand what prompts the question in terms of the reason why it has come to be asked and the issues that accompany it. To do this the following factors need to be taken into account.

1. Firstly, *the historical factor* that contraception has been roundly condemned by the Church throughout its history from Augustine in the fourth century until the remarkable decision of the Lambeth Conference in 1930 to give cautious acceptance.[1] One should ask, why so cautious an acceptance? It sounded as though the Anglican Church was consenting to contraception in the way a parent might anxiously allow a teenage daughter to stay at her first all-night party! Not so much with approval but with resignation and foreboding. This is indicative of the tension in all ecclesiastical authority in carrying out its twin functions of guidance and control. It seems the Church of England was here caught on the horns of a dilemma which was created by a further factor, the technological factor.

2. Secondly, *the technological factor* which refers in this case to the discovery of how to vulcanise rubber in 1843, making the mass production of a reliable and cheap contraceptive possible. Of course it wasn't that there were eighty-seven years of slow growth in production which brought about the Anglican decision so much later; it was simply that 'all-night parties' were clearly here to stay and the modern world had adapted to this invention and its contraceptive potential. Perhaps this is a good example of what Alasdair MacIntyre argued in his lectures on 'Secularisation and Moral Change', that changes in social conditions precede changes in morality. However, it doesn't necessarily follow that this is an inappropriate way for ethical decisions to be made, or that ethical decisions shouldn't allow for considerable future flexibility. But certain types of hierarchical authority and authoritative pronouncements preclude this and it is the Catholic Church that is more often prone to this dilemma than others. (This is not entirely true of course because certain minority Christian traditions, especially of a puritan persuasion, are just as emphatic about the timelessness of their pronouncements and often become more and more separated from the general *mores* of society because of this.)

3. A third influence is *the solidarity factor.* I mean this to refer to the importance of maintaining unity. This was a major concern of Paul in his advice to the Corinthian Church and throughout his mission. The importance of the strong considering their weaker brethren and refraining from certain practices, such as the eating of idol meat, may or may not be appropriate here but the general principle remains: the unity of the brethren as the body of Christ. If the importance of this issue is not understood in studying Christianity, then the character of the tradition will be misunderstood and the reason why its institutions invest authority in different ways will be misinterpreted. Certainly Roman Catholicism is particularly open to misunderstanding for this reason.

4. A fourth influence is *the theological factor.* This helps to explain the distribution of authority by providing a specifically Christian rationale for it. All Christian ethical decisions must have a sound theological basis. This theological basis consists not only of the teaching and acts of Jesus, but also of the doings of the early Church, and by extension the tradition down to the

present day. This idea of tradition, so important in Roman Catholicism, is largely lacking in the lives of many pupils and students. Therefore it is difficult for children to understand that tradition can become a source of authority in itself and that there is a sense in which the revelation of God's Will takes place through it. This notion of agency and the handing-on of authority clearly affects the way ethical decisions are arrived at, but there are few other institutions in modern society in which these notions play so prominent a part. It is out of this tradition that the concept of 'Natural Law' has developed. This means that the creation is seen as God's handiwork which man is not at liberty to disrupt. The causal processes by which it operates are sacrosanct. This way of looking at the universe must be understood before any appreciation of Natural Law can be gained.

Now, with regard to contraception (with the exception of the rhythm method) we have the functioning of natural processes being impeded. So, rejecting contraception becomes an understandable ethical position despite the hardship and emotional stress that, according to other very appealing arguments, this view is said to cause. As to what is right and wrong, that must be decided by means of a further enquiry along the lines of the girl and her fiancé, and it is not the prime task of a study of Catholic ethics to resolve this problem.

The factors listed above relate to the particular example of contraception within Catholicism but the method is valuable for exploring the way in which ethical issues arise within and outside Christianity. The most important point is to be aware of the various influences that produce moral dilemmas. When studying Christianity some of these influences are exclusively Christian, others are more general. It is the merging of the two that may produce a distinctively Christian contribution to a larger debate within society. The notice taken of the Christian debate within society as a whole is a measure of the Church's authority and influence and this is an issue to be explored in the classroom as well.

NOTES

1.   Other Protestant Churches had also given their acceptance but these rulings had less general impact than the Anglican decision.

SECTION C
PRACTICE

12   In the common core, there are many mansions: Teaching Christianity in a multicultural classroom

Angela Wood

I wonder if I'm going mad, I think, as I fight my way across the foyer, struggle up the steps and crawl along the corridor to my classroom....Has this really been decreed as *the* moment to start a new Humanities topic? Is it part of some eternal plan? I know it says on the departmental schedule that it's this week we launch into Christianity and I have been preparing my second years for this moment...but is it *written?* I must say that I'm more than a little apprehensive: the weather is revolting — rainy and grey and cheerless. It affects my moods. It must surely affect the kids; they've been cooped up behind condensation-covered windows all dinner-hour and tempers were running a bit high even this morning. There were one or two social explosions, leading to one or two referrals, and a couple of disciplinary actions. I want to light a candle, not add fuel to the fire...

I'm just making excuses, though, and I have to do it now. What's worrying me is the job itself; *not* the colour of the sky but the nature of the beast. It worries me because it's the first religion our kids 'do' in our Lower School Humanities curriculum. They have a unit early on in the first year called 'What is religion?', a thematic introduction which I like to think of as an exercise in religion-spotting, that provides a way of teasing out the religious dimension implicit in culture. It's hard to tell whether something like that actually *works*...but I sense that it does. They're quite good at picking bits of religious meat from the bones of human life: they did it all their first year. The question now is: can they put flesh on those bones? If they can see religion in culture, can they also see culture in religion? And, more to the point, can these bones live?

I open the door.

'IT'S BETTER OUT THAN IN...'

'Let's see what we get in five minutes — What comes into your head when you think of Christians/Christianity? It can be a list if you like. Yes, you can write in pencil. No, it doesn't matter about spelling. And what's the point of copying what *they've* put? They haven't lived your life, have they? So how can they know what *you* think?'...

That's the key, isn't it? Or rather, it's the gate itself. They're *different*. Now that could be a minus, but I must try to make it into a plus. It means, of course, that I can't really teach this up-front, I mustn't be the leading light! We shall each of us have to light a candle and perhaps light each other's too. And they will be candles of different shapes and sizes and scents. For all human life is here, along the highways and byways of the Edgware Road and the Harrow Road and the Marylebone Flyover. It's hardly the centre of the universe but I'm sure it has a cross-section of the whole world! And it is, too, a place to live for many, beside, not the rivers of Babylon, but the waters of the Grand Union Canal, and even here there are many whose homes are far away and who sit and weep...

If I could have handpicked, I muse, a class-load to teach a Humanities unit on Christianity (three hours a week for half a term) who would I have chosen? Nominal Anglicans? Committed Catholics? Believing Baptists? A mini-WCC? A *tabula rasa* of don't-knows? Would I want them quiet and unquestioning? Defiant and demanding? Or cheerful and challenging? What's the probable composition of the class? At a rough estimate:

Seven Muslims (some Bengali, some Arab, one Turkish, one Moroccan);
Three Roman Catholics (one Italian, one Caribbean, one Irish);
Two Anglicans, friends who've just been confirmed (together);
Two quite intense Pentecostalists;
One very inspiring, with an Elim mother and a Rastaman brother;
One slightly reluctant Greek Orthodox;
One assimilated Sikh, brought up in a Hindu environment;
One confused, with a Muslim father and an agnostic mother;
One Methodist, who might be a lay preacher one day;
One militant Marxist from eastern Europe;
and quite a few who think that 'religion-is-a-load-of-rubbish', plus a fair bit of subliminal superstition and sympathetic magic, and some I confess to not knowing well enough to assess their views.

'DON'T HIDE YOUR LAMP UNDER A BUSHEL...'

So let's see what we've got from the brain-storm. It'll certainly help me to see where they're coming from: will it help them to see where they might be going?

There are a lot of random thoughts, not connected from one individual to another and, in places, it's hard to see how they're connected within an individual. But they *are* connected...they're connected *by* the individual. If we record these publicly, so to speak, on a BB or OHP and each pupil makes his or her own copy, possibly pondering them as they go along, then we can focus on them, unpack them and perhaps rework them a little. We've used this method once or twice before, which is as it should be, because the subject matter is quite difficult enough without having to get used to a different technique. In this case, of course, we'll pretty soon have to differentiate between fact and opinion; perhaps 'experience' is another important category. Some are standard. Some are stereotypes. Some are quite startling:

Bethlehem	monks	bacon
white	stained glass	Adam and Eve
civilised way of life	machine guns	whole world
money	life	Jesus
Big Ben	thieves	Regent Street lights
graves	Romans	church
cross	black and white cloth	tight men
God	bread and wine	Father Christmas and his wife, Merry Christmas
Gospel	turkey	candles
Ash Wednesday	the Pope	deep religion
pork	Bible	'Songs of Praise'
English suits	holly	donations
fairies	Sunday	holy water
money-grabbing	snobby schools	cloaks
resurrection	angels	Christ
baptism	funerals	chapel
Mass	life after death	our teachers

I find it hard to hide my amazement at the business about money — I wonder what the origin of that is — and at the identification of 'Christian' with 'British'. That's easier for me to understand, given that the non-Christians who are definitely something else were none of them born in Britain and so meet British culture and Christianity in one go. Where they came from, there is a higher level of religious conformity or homogeneity and religion is basically inseparable from nationality. They have real trouble seeing the difference. I tell them that I, for example, am British *and* Jewish. 'Oh...'

Off we go. We talk and talk. We could do the whole course like this, I imagine, just wheeling in a bit of evidence and experience — a video here, a worksheet there, a book here, there and everywhere — when it's supportive or stretching. But obviously no one could sustain it that long and I couldn't stand the strain. The rest of the week will do nicely; then we get on to more obviously substantial, 'get-hold-of-able' stuff.

But first, to round this part off and with the permission of the writers it seems appropriate to read to the class parts of some non-list responses which encapsulate so much of what we have been saying.

> I think Christians are like angels and they don't drink and they don't swear and they don't smoke and are always kind to other people they go to church every Sunerday and says there prays Before they go to Bed and listen to Beethoven. (Gemila)

> The first thing I think of is life and people and that is all because I don't believe in Christians. (Rahim)

When I hear the word 'Christian' I don't think of anything. Maybe it's because I don't know very much about them. My mums a Christian. I have no religion. (Darren)

Sometimes I think of Jesus. I think that chriseans are good people. Well most of them anyway. (Emma)

Christianity is a has-been religion. It has done good and evil but is no longer requered. (Wayne)

Through the centuries it has kept the people's spirets and given then cause to live and to fight. On the other hand, the execution has killed thousands. "IN THE NAME OF THE FATHER AND OF THE SON AND OF THE HOLY SPIRIT." (Anna)

Christianity however is not needed enymore. People do not need a god in who's hands to place their destinies in. Christianity is specialy not needed in the age of technology and progress. Christianity stops progress and oposes technology. That is why religion in any way in not needed in the age of progress, aspecialy a religion as wide spread as Christianity. (Kalin)

When I think of christians I think of. I hate christians because in summer In the park they sleep on the grass and in school they fight because they will tell you to give money and one think they like Jesue and they pray for him and In school they fight with us and If you don't give money they will show you a nife and we sked of them and we give them our money that why I hate christians. (Arfat)

'HAVE WE NOT ALL ONE FATHER?'

I'm both excited and anxious about the next bit. We're off to a good start and in a funny sort of way, we've already covered a lot of ground... but we also need to dig deeper, to trace a few patterns of ideas, to draw conclusions which are firmly based, to touch one another's lives — and to take some time to breathe it all in...

It's clear to me that I want to retain both the individual's freedom to 'do his or her own thing' and control of the class as a single unit, that is, maintain both commonality and diversity. I don't have enough inspiration, agility, overview or even stamina to do both at once so it seems better to establish some common ground to start with — not a crash course in Christianity but a shared springboard.

Perhaps the wholeness I'm looking for can be found in the link between the learners and what they are learning, for these kids have seen for themselves that they differ in their perceptions of Christianity. Can they tolerate the idea that *Christians* differ in *their* perceptions of Christianity? It's disturbing for quite a few. Rashid says that you should either be a Christian or not, that Muslims all think the same about Islam so why can't Christians all think the same? Tariq disagrees! Not all Muslims are the same. In his country they have fights because of what they say Islam should be like. Roli wonders if we're being racist...

The time is right for a worked example to get across the idea that Christians are united by certain beliefs but express these in different ways according to culture and experience.

We have the *Believe It or Not* series of videos. A colleague suggests that the one called *Eastern Orthodox* and the one called *Church of England* make a good pair. It's true. We have to show them one at a time, naturally! And with a gap between showings! The best idea is to show the first one with the pupils noting what strikes *them* as significant about that Orthodox Christian community, and then what they think that community might say is significant *about itself.* That's a meal in itself! They come up with things like...the church is like a social club as well as where they can pray; all the work that goes into art; they carry their religion back home from church; when they are in church they are acting out Jesus' life again; they care about each other; and they have their dinner together.

When they come to the *Church of England*, they're not expecting 'another religion' and they don't get one! The differences strike some of them first, then they see the underlying similarities; others see the superficial similarities then find subtle differences. That's exciting in itself!

To pull it together, let's see the *Baptists and Roman Catholics* one. Then I hope we can call this same-but-different business a day, for now anyway. I'm out of school tomorrow so if we tease out as much as we can today they can then tackle a task by themselves. As it happens, it's not a bad way of judging whether they can manage by themselves, of evaluating and reflecting on what's been happening.

'Gosh, Ms, that worksheet you gave us was horrible!' said Lisa. 'You shouldn't use that bright green paper, you know!' (The worksheet is reproduced at the end of this chapter.)

'GO ON YOUR WAY REJOICING!'

There are some members of the class who know exactly where they want to wander. They can draw up a scheme of work quite quickly and set off. Some of them actually want to stay at home, so to speak. That's fine. There is standard pupil-proof coursework, offering a balanced diet of reading, thinking, writing and maybe drawing of different types. It's safe, structured and secure. Then there are some who want to embark on a journey but need a travel agent or perhaps a map-reader.

Quite quickly, certain distinct *modus operandi* are emerging: information-gathering; reviewing and reacting; personal enquiry; creative expression ...They will be using the *modus* which best fits their focus.

Siobhan, an Anglican, wants to know more about C. of E. agencies and charities. I suggest she could study it from an organisational point of view, using some of the methods we developed last year. There's a fair bit of interest in the Turin Shroud. It does seem to be an obvious Humanities topic − 'integrated' within itself, lending itself to open enquiry, developing the ability to work with evidence and apply reason. It appeals to Daniel N.'s scientism. I'm also very glad that Nicola D. is interested in it because she has an aptitude for all the relevant skills and is an independent thinker and worker. She'll bring artistic flair to it, too.

Melanie, fascinated by the Jehovah's Witnesses who get turned away at door after door, wants to understand their motivation and their strategies for survival. I'm not sure you'll find that in normal library books, I tell her. Mind you, we have a wonderful librarian but its still the kind of thing you find out − if at all − by talking to people. If her Mum doesn't want Witnesses to come to the house, she should ask her if she is allowed to do this. I could put her in touch with Witness kids in the school as well as talking to other members of her class.

Luisa wants to research crucifixes and the crucifixion − the different kinds, their origins and significance; the story of the crucifixion of Jesus; how the Romans did it; the styles of the crucifixion in Christian art; what the crucifixion stands for — the image it has left....Gosh! perhaps it should be reduced just a tiny bit...and it would still be very stimulating.

Quite a few are interested or persuaded to take an 'X' view of an aspect of Christianity, e.g. the Muslim view of the crucifixion. Rashid does and doesn't want to. Rachel, some of whose family are Roman Catholic, and Gemila, a Moroccan Muslim, want to collaborate on an aspect of Roman Catholicism, possibly the Pope. Jagjit, known as Bobby, might take a Sikh standpoint about Jesus — not really a comparison with the Gurus....Do you know enough about the Gurus? And Spyros, who struggles with the ancient and the modern in his family and the ancient and the modern in his own mind, is actually going to *study* his own religion and then try to make up his mind....In every case, I insist that they first write down what they *already* think. Then I give them an envelope, and they put what they have written in it and seal it down. It'll be frozen and kept in cold storage till the end of their study so they can see for themselves what the difference is between their views before and after, that is, with and without some serious knowledge!

Bayader has just come to Britain and to this school. We can't speak to each other in English and I do not know her mother tongue, an Arabic dialect. She speaks Sudanese French and I speak British French so we manage a bit. But all our resources on Christianity are in English. She knows the story of Noah, I discover, and I remember that my little girl has a simple reading book about Noah. I would bring it from home for her. She could look at the pictures and learn some English from the writing since she knows the meaning already. I'm not sure that she'll learn anything about Christianity but it's an interesting, reverse process of education. I have a stencil for a 'stained glass window' — at Chichester, coincidentally! — that she might like to colour in. She needs a sense of satisfaction pretty soon, I feel.

David has been struck by many of the posters round the room. In particular, he is fascinated by the CEM poster of the black sculptor producing a black Christ. What is strange about it? Unusual? David cannot speak softly and so the whole class is drawn in into what is becoming for him a personal discovery and a return to his roots.

Nicola M. wants to research Christian beliefs about the afterlife. That's not easy at this level. Maybe it's no bad thing that you absolutely can't pick up a single book and start copying! Omar and Daniel C. want to do images of heaven and hell — 'mental ideas', they say; and if people really believe it's like that. You mean, an opinion poll? Sort of.

Tariq is obsessed by violence, by the idea of violence. He has witnessed political strife in Iran and still gets bits of news. Christians fight, don't they? Are they allowed to have wars? Could he do something about religious wars? He ends up having long chats with the librarian which are good for anyone!

Maurice has decided to check out his Methodist minister, maybe follow him around for a day. The second year is a bit early for work shadowing, isn't it? He'd also like to interview him. He thinks he'd be interesting but his sermons are a bit boring because he nags! Why doesn't *he* write a sermon, then? Does he know about the three-point plan?

There are artists and artists *manqués* and would-be artists in this class. I'm not going to allow the copying of pictures out of books. So how about this: take an event in the life of Jesus and find out what Christians believe about it, how they interpret the evidence and then express what you have discovered in a symbol picture of your own — an original creation? Something along these lines seems to be very acceptable. I added that it was important not just to have Christian ideas 'up in the air' but actually in a form because most Christians believe that Jesus was God in a body. But a straight 'naff' picture won't do because it has to show certain, special ideas. The point is that Jesus is believed to have been human but not an ordinary human. Kiya wants to do pictures of ideas of Jesus — Messiah, Son of God — which is surprising as he takes a very strict Muslim line on so many things. Did he realise...? Yes, it's all right. It's also surprising that he wants to skip his Maths and Languages lessons to do more of his pictures in the lessons when I'm free. Rui also wants to spend extra time on his ideas — pictures of the miracles that Jesus performed. Rahim is toying with the idea of Christian values and 'things which are good', e.g. love or peace. I like Tina and Germaine's idea of the birth, death and resurrection of Jesus — those key experiences! A triptych form seems appropriate but I'm anxious about it being sustained. That anxiety fades into insignificance as a more pressing issue develops. How to portray Jesus? No one knows exactly what Jesus looks like but I hint that he might possibly have had features like Anwarul's. Germaine says Jesus is blond in all the pictures they have at home and, anyway, if you can have a black Jesus, why can't you have an English Jesus? Jesus isn't a country, Sawkat says softly. I'm glad someone's got the point. Alfred announces proudly and loudly that he's black British. A heated discussion ensues about the ethnicity of Jesus and the universality of Christ, I need to inject the odd fact...but there's no way to resolve the matter. As a working hypothesis, I suggest that the points Germaine wants to get across could be made by giving each of the three figures a different 'racial' type, like the Three Wise Men in many nativities. Tina goes one further: why don't they do all the 'Jesuses medium'...?

Roli and Alfred are doing something they say is a secret. It gives me grey hairs to think about it but I try to make myself believe that it will be 'all right on the night' even though there is no clear evidence of any real organisation. It's something to do with stars. As in Hollywood? No, as in Bethlehem!

BAUBLES, BANGLES AND BLACK AND WHITE POSTERS

It is a short but well-established tradition in the school that the foyer be decorated for Christmas a few weeks beforehand. Custom seems to favour the Christmas tree, hung with empty presents! The decorations tend to be of the tinselly variety and I am anxious to suggest that there are other approaches to Christmas, that it means something which transcends the commercialism, and indeed, that it is one of the finest and highest expressions of Christian values.

Last summer I bought some of those stunning 'quotation posters' depicting 'real life' scenes interpreted by a biblical phrase, poem or extract from a modern Christian's speech. Seventy of these are up on the black and white and grey marble-clad walls at the entrance to the school. They are there, affixed harmlessly with 'Copydex', and I intend them to establish a deeper, more thoughtful and sensitive mood. I am hoping that with the advent of the tinsel and baubles, the two approaches will blend aesthetically but challenge each other ideologically. They are mostly there as a teaching resource for the second years studying Christianity this half-term but others who pass through the foyer are free to look at them: actually, they're not really free *not* to as the posters are so compelling.

Fahid and Kalin, a Muslim and a Marxist respectively, are the best of friends despite their daily squabbles. There are times when the basic difference of life-stance is immaterial; times when it's painful; times when they just don't know how to tackle it. Something that might be helpful is a serious poster-viewing session as a focus or a vehicle for a discussion. Some of the posters seem to be definitely Christological in words or pictures or both; some are broadly humanistic. I set them the task of listing those which are, respectively, 'Christian only' and 'possibly Muslim'; and 'Christian only' and 'possibly Marxist' — with reasons, of course; then to compare lists but not to force a consensus.

'MY CHILD THAT WAS LOST MAY HAVE FOUND SOMETHING...'

I originally thought that we'd have some sort of formal reporting-back session after the 'Go on your way, rejoicing' phase — like those slide shows after the school trip. As it turned out, the process was quite public most of the time and there has been a fair bit of cross-fertilisation and free advice floating around. Some pieces have been fairly individual and these can now be shared.

> I think Christianity is a very big and known religion. I have learned a lot about Jesus...but I still don't think I know enough about Christianity...First I never knew about Jesus, only God and I thought that Jesus was God's son. Now I know for some people Jesus runs their lives, like the ones in Wallsingham. For me, I pray to not just one god but three or four gods. Sometimes I think God is cruel because people are suffering for example the famine in Ethiopia. And for all the diseases there are in the world. (Jagjit/Bobby)
>
> I don't really like Orthodox church because when I get there it's all right and lighting the candles and kissing the pictures of crist but when it comes to praying I don't really like that because I don't know any prays. I do like easter when we light candles all the way from morning till night. I make patterns on the soft wax. When we come back home we crack red eggs and the strongest egg gets placed next to the holy fire which we call kandila. We leave it there for one year then when the year passes we chuck the rotten egg into a lake or river and replace. (Spyros)
>
> The reason why I think the sculptor was carving a black christ is because christ was born over 2000 years ago when there were not many white people in Africa.
>
> I saw a programme about Africa which showed me what happened 2000 years ago, the pictures were of the black Madonna and black baby.
>
> Christ was a Jew and the Jews were descended from Ethiopa which were prominently

black in those days, so I think it would be almost impossible for Christ to be white in those days.

The sculptor will naturally do black people or he may be tired of all the white Christ and just decided to do a black one instead. Maybe Christ was not black, but he was not white either. Like in white people's case many of them think that everythink white is good and everythink black is bad. In his mind he might think everythink black is good and everythink white is evil. (David)

A CHRISTMAS MEANING CAKE

To wrap it up in the last week of term, which is the last week of this unit and the last week before Christmas, we bake ourselves a cake. We freely-associate about Christmas and group our ideas into customs associated with Christmas (Santa Claus, cards, gifts, turkeys, trees, etc.); the story of the birth of Jesus (wise men, shepherds, donkeys, Gabriel, stable, etc.); and the purpose or meaning of Christmas — what it's trying to say (peace, love, eternal life, getting close to God, incarnation, etc.). We can soon see that you get the customs first — some people don't go any further — then you might know the story of Jesus' birth. But what it's all about is the love and the incarnation bit. We're putting this into the layers of a cake (in drawing or models): the icing is the customs, the marzipan is the story and the cake itself is the meaning...

THE PARTY'S OVER

It's the last day of the term and Christmas hasn't happened yet but the decorations must come down. The marble-clad walls must be returned to their pristine, 'Copydex'-free state. Many hands make light work. 'You're lucky there's no graffiti, Ms!' Indeed, one must be grateful for small mercies such as that! There are a few splashes of red wine, no doubt from last night's staff party, but that is surely not indicative of anything...

'I've gotta go now, Ms, Mary Christmas!' (Ha! Ha!)

'Mary Christmas, Joseph!'

BAPTISTS AND ROMAN CATHOLICS

Using the notes you made on the video you saw yesterday, draw out the *differences* you can find between Baptists and Roman Catholics. You can do it like a chart if you like by copying the following into your folder and filling it in and carrying on:

(continued over)

Baptists	Roman Catholics
1. Baptism by immersion in a special pool.	Baptism by pouring water on the head.
2. Baptism only of teenagers upwards because...	Baptism of babies
3. At Communion, bread...	....
4.	Bread given individually by priest or lay person
5. Grape juice	Wine mixed with...
6. drunk from...	People come up to the altar
7. Children...	Children...
8. Minister dressed in...	Priest dressed in...

Try to think of *two* more points of comparison to make *ten* altogether.
2. Look again at your notes and pick out as many similarities (things which are the same) as you can. Look for beliefs, actions, thoughts, feelings, sounds, appearances — anything which seems to show that Roman Catholics and Baptists have a lot in common.

Write down or draw (on plain paper) these similarities.
3. One of the similarities is the use of water. You saw Baptists being baptised and you saw Roman Catholics dipping their finger in holy water and making the sign of the Cross.

Water is symbolic: it stands for an idea or a feeling. What do you think it stands for? (Answer as fully as you can.)
4. Draw and describe three or more things you saw in the video which interested you. Say why they interested you. If you like, comment on those things...say if you agree or disagree and why.

This is to be started in class and finished for homework. See you next Tuesday.

      A. Wood   (15.11.84)

13 A long day at the Vatican

Nora Horrigan

What you are about to read is an account of an hour-long lesson which was based on a method gleaned from the educationalist Douglas Barnes (*From Communication to Curriculum,* Harmondsworth, Penguin Books, 1976), and which was taught, successfully, to all levels of ability in the third year of a comprehensive school. It is suggested that the reader tries out the lesson, studies the methodology which underlies it, and then works on the follow-up suggestions. The methodology is described briefly at the end of this article, but it can be found in more detail in the books recommended for further reading.

THE LESSON

The basis for the lesson is an extract taken from Jennings, P. and McCabe, E. 1982 *The Pope in Britain*, London, Bodley Head.

Introduction

Most pupils have heard about the Pope, and some are aware that he has both religious and political influence. This lesson seeks to do more than merely teach about the Pope. The extract relating to him is used as a starting-point for a journey from the border to a part of the interior of Christianity.

Stage one – the topic is presented to the whole class

(a) Each pupil is given a copy of the extract which is printed below.
(b) The extract is read by either a good reader in the class, or by the teacher.

It is of note that it is a topic to which each person can relate — a day in a life.

A long day at the Vatican

The Pope usually begins his day at 5.30am. He is frequently in his small chapel by 6am, where he spends an hour in prayer and meditation before saying Mass. While eating breakfast, the Pope reads the major Italian newspapers. He works in his study until 11am, writing, dictating and correcting documents and speeches. In 1979, his first full year in office, he is said to have delivered over five hundred addresses.

The rest of the morning is devoted to private audiences with cardinals, bishops, visiting Heads of State, ambassadors, and people from every kind of organisation and walk of life. The Pope often has 'working lunches', and if there are no guests he is joined by his two private secretaries. Lunch is prepared and served by the Polish Sisters who look after the Pope's apartment; it usually takes the form of his favourite Polish dishes, especially when Polish guests are present, although he also eats Italian and other Western food.

Despite his already very long and full day, Pope John Paul does not usually take a siesta, preferring instead to relax by walking in the Vatican gardens or up and down the terraces of the Apostolic Palace above his private apartment. Sometimes as he walks on the terrace he recites the Rosary, or reads. The Pope is fond of singing and music. He also loves to swim when he can, and has a swimming pool built at his summer residence about fifteen miles outside Rome.

During the afternoon the Pope works in his study for two or three hours. He often continues with private audiences for his advisers or people he was unable to fit in during the morning.

For his dinner the Pope prefers a simple, light meal, especially when he is dining alone or with his secretaries. He may watch the television news while he is eating. He loves meeting people, and on occasions he invites friends to supper at the Vatican, often joining in a sing-song afterwards.

Pope John Paul II then spends several more hours working in his study, reading letters and documents. He retires to bed very late, rarely before 1am, *having first spent a long period in prayer in his private chapel.*

(Jennings, P. and McCabe, E. (1982) *The Pope in Britain*, London, Bodley Head)

(c) Pupils' immediate reactions are elicited by the teacher asking such questions as, 'What are your impressions of the Pope?' and 'How does his day compare with your own?' Lively discussion is recommended!

Stage two — the pupils are expected to explore the material for themselves and to talk about the issues to which their attention has been directed

(a)   Pupils are asked to work in pairs.
(b)   Each pair is to discuss the following questions:
1.   What can you learn about the Pope from this account?
2.(i)   What do you know about prayer?
   (ii)   Why, in your opinion, does the Pope spend so much of his precious time in prayer?
   (iii)   What, if anything, do you know about the rosary?

Stage three – the teacher refocuses attention, and not only develops knowledge, but also engages the pupil in the rather lonely task of writing

(a)   Pupils' points about the Pope are collected.

(b)   Further information is given about John Paul II (see Schools Council (1981) *What is the Christian Church?*, Surrey Fine Art Press, pp.39–40), and about how a pope is chosen (the black and white smoke is generally of particular interest!).

(c)   Each pupil is then issued with half a sheet of exercise paper and asked to write his/her own answer to question 2(i) on one side, and question 2(ii) on the other. Names are not required and secrecy is requested. Sufficient time is allowed to enable them to write thoughtful answers.

Stage four – the written work is shared and, it is hoped, understanding developed

(a)   Pupils are asked to make columns in their notebooks like the ones illustrated below. Each number represents a pupil in the class.

Fair	Fairly Good	Good
1.		
2.		
3. and so on		

(b)   The teacher then reads out half the answers to question 2(i) and then half the answers to question 2(ii). Anonymity is protected and pupils are asked not to reveal their identities as their work is read. What they are asked to do is to assess each piece of work by ticking the appropriate column. This both assures their attention and gives them a part in the evaluation process.

Examples of some pupil responses are outlined below
Selected answers to question 2(i)

> Prayer is a way of speaking to God privately. Some people find it comforting when they are worried or frightened. Perhaps they have done something wrong and they feel when they pray their sin has been forgiven.

> Prayer is often used for saying 'thank you' or asking God for help. Prayers can be said by anyone, anywhere, they do not have to be said or read in a church or other place of worship. Many people think that prayer is stupid today. However, in some ways when you have said prayers you feel relieved. I never usually pray but when I do, it is mostly when I am in trouble.

> Prayer is a way of talking to God. It is also a way of thinking deeply about yourself and others.

Prayer is usually said in a chapel or a church. People of any religion do it and this means to them that they can communicate with God. A prayer is a sort of religious poem. There are different sorts of prayer.

Selected answers to question 2(ii)

The Pope spends so much of his time in private prayer because it is a part of his duty to serve God. It probably helps to give him the strength to work long hours. Also, he has a lot to pray about.

I think that the Pope spends so much of his life in private prayer away from other people because he feels that he is speaking to God alone and that nobody else can intrude. He obviously prefers praying in private.

The Pope, as head of the Catholic Church, has responsibility for its people. He needs to try to know God's will and to be able to interpret it. He has an exacting life and needs to draw strength from God.

I think that the Pope spends so much of his time in private prayer to talk to God and to calm his nerves in relation to the unfortunate things which have happened to him during the day, and to relax him after a strenuous day.

(c)   Answers with the most ticks under 'Good' are rewarded and read again. It is noteworthy that the final stage of this lesson produces both excitement and involvement. It is rather good if time almost runs out as the pupils generally want to finish even if the bell has gone.

Stage five – a time for reflection and the reinforcement of that which has been learned

Pupils take home their answers to question 2(i) and 2(ii), improve them, and then write them up in their notebooks.

CONCLUSION

In the introduction it was stated that the material in this lesson was to be used to take the pupils 'from the border to a part of the interior of Christianity'. It is hoped that the work done has not only revealed to the pupils facts (some surprising) about the Pope, but that it has also drawn them into discovering something of the significance of prayer in Christian experience.

Follow-up suggestions

1.   The pupils' knowledge of the rosary, question 2(iii), could be explored and developed. (See Rankin, J. (1982) *Christian Worship* pp.12–13 Cambridge, Lutterworth Press.) Also, use firsthand experience. For example, a nun was asked why she used the rosary. Her reply?

I know that it takes me forty minutes to go round the whole rosary, so I set that time aside and then I don't think about time at all during my prayer period. I suppose that as well as reminding us of Jesus, the use of a rosary is a means of calming my body and stilling my mind.

2.   Christian prayers could be examined which are, for example, a part of Christian rites of passage, or meditative prayers like those contained in Quoist, M. (1963) *Prayers of Life,* Dublin, Gill & Son.

3.   The meaning of the following extract could be discussed.

> He was a simple old sailor, the skipper of the small boat that was taking them to the Shetlands, and they were a young, lively party, actors and actresses from London on tour, going to do a night or two on the Islands. They were not above 'taking the mickey' a bit, and they thought his way of saying grace before meals very quaint and old-fashioned. However, before long a storm blew up, a really severe north-easter, and as the ship began to pitch more and more violently, morale among the visitors got lower and lower.
>
> A small deputation went up to ask the Captain's opinion. 'Well,' he said, 'maybe we'll get through, and maybe we won't. I never remember such a storm.' The news was greeted with dismay below, and finally another deputation went up to the bridge to ask whether perhaps the Captain would be so good as to come and say a prayer with his terrified passengers. His reply was simple: 'I say my prayers when it's calm; and when it's rough, I attend to my ship.' (Campling, C. and Davis, M. (eds.) (1969) *Words for Worship*, London, Edward Arnold)

4.   Styles of Christian worship could be explored, for example, Eastern Orthodoxy, Pentecostal, Salvation Army. (See John Rankin's *Christian Worship* in the Chichester Project series.)

5.   An understanding of the use of silence in worship could be gained from an in-depth study of the Society of Friends. (See Gorman, G. (1977) *The Society of Friends,* Exeter, Religious and Moral Education Press.) The list is endless, but care needs to be taken with both the choice of material and the methods of presentation, if boredom is not to set in. It is with methods of presentation that the final section of this article is concerned.

THE METHODOLOGY

The lesson outlined on the previous pages is based on a method which respects the pupils' autonomy, values their knowledge and gains their involvement. It breaks away from a rigid and formal way of teaching where the teacher's prime use of language is a one-way communication, merely passing on information, expecting only to receive it back correctly understood. Here the use of language is planned so that the pupils can recode the lesson material for themselves and reflect upon it. This method of teaching in no way causes the teacher to abrogate his/her responsibilities. The curriculum is pupil-related, rather than child- or subject-centred. It is something to be mastered and understood, and it is concerned with focused and systematic activity and not aimless discussion.

BOOKS RECOMMENDED FOR FURTHER READING

Smart, N. (1979) *The Phenomenon of Christianity,* London, Collins

Barnes, D. (1976) *From Communication to Curriculum,* Harmondsworth, Penguin Books

Barnes, D. and Todd, F. (1977) *Communication and Learning in Small Groups,* London, Routledge & Kegan Paul Ltd.

14 Mottoes and morality: Christian ethics in the classroom

David Minton

(An outline of work on the moral aspect of Christianity based on the idea of 'mottoes')

The aim of this outline is to help children acquire some understanding of ethics in general and of Christian ethics in particular. Individual elements of the outline have been used at one or more of the levels in the secondary school age range and, with appropriate adaptation, the idea as a whole could be considered for use especially with pupils from the age of thirteen to eighteen. I am including very little in the way of pupil reaction or pupil work since I am writing from the memory of lessons conducted over the last eighteen years. I shall, however, try to be concrete enough in my suggestions for the reader to be able to apply them to the practicalities of his or her own situation.

The idea of 'mottoes' is chosen as the key to the outline since, on the one hand, the actual word and notion of 'ethics' have little meaning for most pupils and, on the other hand, the word 'motto' bears several everyday connotations in the mind and experience of the pupil. It also has the merit of fitting in with various approaches to and aspects of the subject of Christian ethics:

(a)   the introduction to and definition of ethics in general;
(b)   the comparison of ethical emphases in different religions;
(c)   the history of moral standpoints in world culture and in the biblical and Christian traditions;
(d)   the question of what is distinctively Christian in Christian ethics, including the understanding of particular teachings of Jesus;
(e)   the challenge to the individual pupil to discover and develop his or her own stance.

The aspects on which I have concentrated in my own work and in this article are the first, (a) 'Introduction to Ethics', the third, (c) 'Mankind's Search for Morality', and the fourth, (d) 'What is specially Christian about Christian Ethics?'

INTRODUCTION TO ETHICS

The theme should be introduced in a manner appropriate to the group, brain-storming the whole business of mottoes, maxims and slogans. For the purpose of the introduction, the words 'motto', 'maxim' and 'slogan' (or 'logo') are given separate senses, despite the overlappings of meaning that occur in general usage, but I have found this a helpful procedure.

Mottoes

Knights of old had mottoes. Towns, countries, some schools and a wide variety of other organisations have mottoes. Pupils in pairs or small groups can make a list of things that they know have mottoes and try to remember the mottoes themselves. They can consider what purpose the mottoes serve.

A motto expresses the value of its holder. It contains an aim or a programme for action. The Scout Movement has the motto, 'Be Prepared!' There are many different levels on which it can be applied — being prepared for emergencies, for outdoor living, for adventure, to help other people and to survive. The motto also contains a scale of values. Someone who goes camping without a knife is to be criticised. Someone who goes mountaineering with a first-aid kit is to be praised. This is the beginning of the difficult idea of 'ethics'. An ethic is a scale of values to do with action. Ethics are the ideas or points of conscience which people refer to when they say that an act is good or bad. They are your way of life from the point of view of moral value. Scouts approve of preparedness and disapprove of unpreparedness.

Maxims

The word 'maxim' is a useful label for a personal motto which may often be unsaid. It is the motto which is proclaimed, not by our words, but by our actions and, as we say, actions speak louder than words. Everybody has a maxim, whether they like it or not, and whether they realise it or not. If people live entirely selfishly, then their maxim is 'Me first'. That may not be their motto. They might be scouts, officially dedicated to helping other people at all times, but their actual selfish way of life, their maxim, gives the lie to their motto. Pupils in pairs can tell each other what they think their own maxim is and what they think that of the other pupil is.

Slogans

A slogan is something shouted or printed on a T-shirt. Slogans are perhaps associated more with football matches, demonstrations and advertisements, but some are ethical. An advertiser starting a campaign for a new product looks for a good 'logo', so what are a person's (or a religion's) ethics, but that person's (or that religion's) 'logo for life'?

Classwork and discussion

Pupils can be encouraged to produce their own examples of mottoes, maxims and slogans. They could then consider the following list. Into which of the three categories do these statements fit? What do the pupils think of them?
1. Might is right
2. Look after number one
3. Charity begins at home
4. Honesty is the best policy
5. The customer is always right
6. Pull up the ladder, Jack, I'm all right
7. The survival of the fittest
8. It's love that makes the world go round
9. Others first
10. Live for kicks

Does the school have a motto? If so, what is it? If not, what would the pupils choose? Pupils can be asked to think of a 'logo for life' for their T-shirts. They can then be asked to think of a maxim which would make the world a better place if it were put into practice by everybody. For example, 'Never be the first to fight.' What would the world be like if everyone stuck to that maxim?

MANKIND'S SEARCH FOR MORALITY

Over thousands of years, and around the world, people have produced different ideas of justice and different codes of behaviour. They are in part a progressive development in history but also in part live options for anybody at any time.

Escalation

The law of the jungle. You steal my chicken, I steal your cow. You kill my slave, I kill your son. You give me a black eye, I break your nose. You steal my compass, I take your pencil case. What is right about escalation? Does it teach the offender a lesson? Does it make him more bitter? What is wrong with escalation?

Retaliation

Levelling up. Calling it quits. Eye for eye, tooth for tooth, hand for hand, foot for foot. (Exodus 21:24). Although this may look to us 'primitive' and like 'rough justice', in human history it was often a step forward from the principle of escalation or the law of the jungle. When it was first said, 'an eye for an eye' really meant 'no more than an eye for an eye'. If someone knocks one of your teeth out, you don't knock out ten of his, just one.

Pupils can be asked to think of any other points in favour of 'an eye for an eye': at least it gives the other person a dose of his own medicine without giving him an excuse to level up further; at least it teaches the other person what it feels like to be treated the way he treated you. Can pupils think of any points against 'an eye for an eye'? Does it justify capital punishment — 'a life for a life'?

Reciprocity

Generally speaking one can say that the main ethical systems that have developed in religions, including Christianity, from the idea of retaliation, have all been versions of a related idea, that of 'reciprocity'. I am assuming here that ethics are essentially a social matter, but this itself could be discussed in the classroom. Does a solitary survivor on a desert island have any ethical problems at all? Even the issue of keeping alive to be rescued is a social one, since to be rescued is to return to society. Suicide in society is an ethical problem, in that one is depriving other people of one's existence. But on a desert island? Suicide on a desert island might be a *religious* or *spiritual* problem, but is it an *ethical* one? What is the difference?

Taking ethics, then, as primarily a social issue, one can say that it is about 'me' and 'others' (or 'my neighbour'). Are the three 'I's with which most ethics seem to start (injustice, injury and insult) to follow a pattern of escalation or retaliation or reciprocity?

What is reciprocity? There are three versions of it which can be compared in the classroom — those of Confucius, Christ and Kant. Each of these is put by its proponent in terms of a motto.

The Silver Rule of Confucius

In the fifth century BC, Confucius was asked in China, 'Is there any one word that can serve as a principle for the conduct of life?' Confucius answered, 'Perhaps the word is reciprocity, do not do to others what you would not want others to do to you.' (*Analects* XV:23) Here we have a single word and a motto. The word 'reciprocity' needs to be explained in the classroom, something which can best be done by using the idea of thoughts in people's heads. In 'escalation' a person is thinking, 'How can I get ahead of the other person?' or 'How can I put one across him?' In retaliation, a person is thinking, 'How can I get my own back?' In 'reciprocity' a person is thinking, 'Suppose the other person were me?' The teacher should bring out the point that Confucius used reciprocity in a negative way. He suggested that in our dealings with others we should think, 'Would I like such and such done to me? No? In which case I should not do it to others.' Each pupil can be asked for an example of a 'negative reciprocal motto' or 'NO-LOGO'. The resulting discussion should

produce such ideas as:
    You don't like to be sworn at. Don't swear at others.
    You don't like to be taken for granted. Don't take others for granted.
    You don't like to be hit. Don't hit others.
    You don't like to be shouted at. Don't shout at others.
    You don't like to be 'put down'. Don't 'put down' others.
    The class could be asked to consider if there is a similar list for nations as distinct from individuals. What sort of society would result from a serious effort by the majority to apply negative reciprocity?

The Golden Rule of Christ

Christians called negative reciprocity the Silver Rule in comparison with Jesus' teaching of positive reciprocity, the Golden Rule: 'Do unto others as you would have them do unto you.' (Luke 6:31, Matthew 7:12) Classwork on example applications of the Golden Rule should produce such suggestions as:
    You would like others to help you. Help them.
    You would like others to listen to you. Listen to them.
    You would like others to respect you. Respect them.
    You would like others to be friendly to you. Be friendly to them.
    The teacher might feel it appropriate to consider snags or pitfalls of the Silver and Golden Rules. Would the Silver Rule produce a peaceful but also passive society? Would the Golden Rule produce a philanthropic but pragmatic society in which people do good in order to have good done to them, a society which would breed such mottoes as 'Honesty is the best policy', 'The customer is always right', 'Enlightened self-interest' and 'Righteousness pays!'?

The 'ends and means' idea of Immanuel Kant

At the end of the eighteenth century the German philosopher, Kant, suggested what is perhaps the most complicated version of reciprocity. Having made the point which we have already noted, that all people have a maxim, whether they know it or not, Kant suggested that the best test of a good maxim was to see if the person holding it would mind if it were used back on him or her. That is the test of reciprocity. People with a maxim like, 'Tread on other people's toes in order to get to the top of the ladder' would probably be the first to squeal if that maxim were used on them. It is therefore a bad maxim. The class could be encouraged to suggest and discuss maxims which may be 'bad' in this sense, e.g. the maxim of a cannibal, or a sadist, or a thief, or perhaps of a nation with nuclear weapons. Kant then went on to give his own suggestion of a maxim which the holder would be quite happy to have reciprocated, and the universal application of which would make the world a better place. This he called the 'Categorical Imperative'. That is, 'Treat other people as ends in themselves and not as means to your ends.' Don't treat other people as stepping-stones to your own goal. Treat them as people who have goals of their own. If that were my maxim, I should be very happy to have it reciprocated. Pupils should be encouraged to suggest, discuss or even act out examples of both the application and the infringement of this principle.

WHAT IS SPECIALLY CHRISTIAN ABOUT CHRISTIAN ETHICS?

Many years ago the BBC Reith lectures had the title, 'The Englishness of English Art'. We talk of English painters and have exhibitions of English paintings, but what is specially English about English art apart from the nationality of the artists? Is there anything? One might similarly ask, 'What is the Christian-ness of Christian ethics?'

A first way in which this question can be approached in the classroom is through the *parables* of Jesus. Most pupils who have some knowledge of Christianity have heard of Jesus' parables, in general, and of the Good Samaritan, in particular. After a recapitulation of the parable of the Good Samaritan, perhaps through updated versions supplied by members of the class, the teacher can suggest mottoes for the main protagonists:

The motto of the thieves: 'What's mine is mine, and what's yours is mine, if I can get it.'

The motto of those who passed by: 'What's mine is mine, and what's yours is yours, if you can keep it.'

The motto of the Good Samaritan: 'What's yours is yours, and what's mine is yours and you can have it.'

Which of these mottoes is the more Christian, and why?

Other parables could be offered to the class for similar treatment. What would be the motto of each protagonist in the parable of the Prodigal Son — the younger son, the father, the older son? Which is the more Christian and why?

A second way to help pupils to understand the Christian-ness of Christian ethics is through the *precepts* of Jesus, especially in the Sermon on the Mount (Matthew 5, 6 and 7) and the Sermon on the Plain (Luke 6:20-49). One exercise could be based on the Beatitudes which are mottoes of a kind. Pupils individually or in small groups could be asked to write ten mottoes starting with the words 'Happy are those who...' Answers might well include such contributions as:

those who have enough money to buy whatever they want

those who are world-famous

those who have great power

those who always win

those who have all they want to eat and drink

A comparison with the Beatitudes in Matthew will then show the difference between the values taught by Jesus and those accepted at large in today's world. The point comes over even more strongly if pupils then look at the 'Woes' or the 'Miserable are those who...' in Luke 6, especially in a modern version. Our society's picture of a happy person turns out to be Jesus' picture of a miserable person. Why?

Another element of Christian ethics which can be taught through the precepts of Jesus is idealism. This is found especially in those passages in which Jesus used the formula, 'You have heard that it has been said...but I say unto you.' In contrast with traditional religious morality as exemplified in the Law of or the 'Miserable are those who...' in Luke 6, especially in a modern version. Moses, the specifically Christian note is sounded in that which follows 'but I say unto you.' Pupils could be encouraged to make a collection of such statements from Matthew 5. A good example is that in verses 38 and 39 which takes the pupils back to the theme of retaliation:

> You have heard it said 'An eye for an eye and a tooth for a tooth', but I say to you that you do not resist evil, but whoever hits you on your right cheek, turn to him the other also.

These words in my experience horrify the teenager of the last quarter of the twentieth century in a way which they did not horrify school pupils of the third quarter. The majority voice in youth culture now celebrates 'hardness' and despises 'softness' and the teacher has to help pupils to see that it is 'hard' to be 'soft' like Jesus, to turn the other cheek and to repay evil with good.

Thus our classroom search for the distinctive Christian ethic takes us finally from the *Parables* and the *Precepts* to the *Passion* of Jesus. The Christian ethic is ultimately the ethic of the Cross and the teacher can meet the horrified reaction of pupils to Matthew 5:39 by saying, 'If we want to see this in action, we must look at the Cross.'

After the account of the Passion and Crucifixion of Jesus has been recapitulated, pupils can be asked to suggest any motto which expresses the ethic of these events. One which could be fed into the discussion is that which Harry S. Truman is said to have had on his desk when he was President of the United States: 'The buck stops here.' In context, this motto presumably expressed both the President's ultimate responsibility to carry the burden of a national problem and also the lack of anyone in a higher office to whom he could 'pass the buck'. However, if one assumes that the buck (or dollar) that everyone wants to pass on is a false one, then it becomes a symbol of all the false currency, so to speak, in human affairs. No one wants to be caught with the fake buck or the hot potato, or the 'bad vibrations' at the end of the game or, so to speak, the parcel when the music stops. The trader who is paid a large sum for a commodity in forged notes and decides not to pass them onto anyone else has taken that loss onto himself. That, in worldly and convential wisdom, is foolishness, but it is the essential Christian ethic. The ethic of the Cross is to take the loss or the evil in a situation onto oneself, thus saving others from it. It is to take the violence and vindictiveness out of a situation by absorbing them and not letting them bounce off onto someone else. Whether teenage pupils in the society of the last quarter of the twentieth century AD will find it easy to understand that is a moot point, but at least this outline aims to help them try.

NOTES

1. The Golden Rule

Whether such precepts in the Sermon on the Mount are for practice *now* (ethic of the realised kingdom) or a description of a dispensation yet to come (futurist eschatology, leaving need for an *interim* ethic) is not of primary relevance to the article. Pupils were asked to show comprehension of the precept (realisable or not) in terms of its 'logo'. My main interest was a comparison with the other mottoes in the sequence (from Hammurabi to Kant) for their different postures in the basic 'me and my neighbour' area of ethics.

15 Reading pictures and understanding Christian experience

Clive Erricker

This article considers the use of art and visual material in the teaching of Christianity to enhance our understanding of religious experience. I believe it does so for the following reasons:

(a) pictures often help to evoke the feeling of an experience and are often a more stimulating and acceptable focus for response than the written word;

(b) when used together, stories and pictures can often enliven the imagination more readily than either alone;

(c) the use of more than one medium often makes the understanding of another's experience more accessible because links with our own experience can be more easily established.

Two criteria should be stressed concerning this approach. Firstly, that there are different types of visual art just as there are different types of literature and to understand correctly the pupil must be aware of what type of art he is looking at and therefore what intention it has. Secondly, that art, in common with all human expression, must be approached with openness. For example, the question 'What is it trying to say?' as a means of appraisal should take priority over the judgement 'Do I like it?' in seeking an understanding of a work of art.

AVOIDING CARICATURE

This is such an important point that it has to be dealt with in advance. Caricature, like stereotyping, results from seeing others as being representatives of a type. But implicit in caricature is a judgement based on preference. We caricature those we do not consider worthy of understanding. It is an

impoverished view because it sees others in accordance with the importance (or rather lack of importance) they have within our own mythology, rather than as they see themselves.

Pictures 3—6 illustrate just this. Each is a caricature of a certain type of person who can be classified within a caricatured Christian framework. This is part of their humour but we must accept that we are looking at cartoons and caricaturing is of the essence of cartoon expression. We must not read into the cartoon form a serious analysis of Christians and Christianity because this is not their intention. Nevertheless, it is often the case that popular media portrayals, especially in visual form , as for example in television programmes, present us with a caricature of clergy, etc.

UNDERSTANDING REPRESENTATION

If the difference between caricature and representation is not learned in dealing with the cartoons (Pictures 3—6) then Picture 7 will be wholly misunderstood.

Grant Wood's *American Gothic* might be treated as a caricature if approached in the wrong spirit, but in fact it is not; it is a distilled impression. That is to say, it concentrates the qualities of the early American Puritan settlers. It is not a snapshot taken by a passer-by, therefore the way the picture happens to be is not the result of a chance encounter, it is representative and symbolic. In approaching the picture this must be understood. How is this to be conveyed to the pupils? They must be aware that we are looking at the mythology of the Puritan settlers as represented in the couple: their attitudes, their way of life — everything in the picture is designed to convey this. Unlike the caricature we are seeing them as they see themselves, as interpreted by the artist, but we must do them, and the artist, justice. A suitable question is, 'What are they saying to us?' It is likely that the student will feel confronted by the couple, almost judged. When prompted to ask questions about the couple, pupils often respond with questions like 'Why are they so unhappy?' which is, of course, merely a subjective interpretation of the facial expressions of those portrayed. What device can best overcome this problem and demonstrate the importance of understanding differences in perceptual procedure in relation to different interpretations of gestures, words and other 'signifiers'? One useful device is for the teacher to be the couple: he speaks for them as the representative of their kind. Once pupils accept the teacher as authoritative in this role the difficulties posed by their differing uninformed interpretations are overcome.

The sort of understanding I wish to bring out by this method is as follows:

There is a great deal of background to be explained in terms of the American settler such as, for example, the religious views they held that persuaded them to leave countries like England, and seek a new life in another country in which they would have freedom to establish a society based on *their* principles. But, of course, the kind of life they had led was also economically conditioned. So there was a connection between their lack of wealth, their hard work and their vulnerability to the vicissitudes of nature. This provides an echo of the

Picture 7 American Gothic by Grant Wood (Picture by courtesy of the Art Institute of Chicago)

Genesis story of the Fall which was seen by them to be a true model of the way things are. In other words, despite its hardship they felt spiritually at home in this 'exile'. Pupils can then read the Genesis story, as printed here:

Then the Lord God planted a garden in Eden, in the East, and there he put the man he had formed. He made all kinds of beautiful trees grow there and produce good fruit. In the middle of the garden stood the tree that gives life and the tree that gives knowledge of what is good and what is bad....

Then the Lord God placed the man in the Garden of Eden to cultivate it and guard it. He said to him, 'You may eat the fruit of any tree in the garden, except the tree that gives knowledge of what is good and what is bad. You must not eat the fruit of that tree; if you do, you will die the same day.'

Then the Lord God said, 'It is not good for the man to live alone. I will make a suitable companion to help him.' So he took some soil from the ground and formed all the animals and all the birds. Then he brought them to the man to see what he would name them; and that is how they all got their names. So the man named all the birds and all the animals; but not one of them was a suitable companion to help him. Then the Lord God...formed a woman out of the man's rib and brought her to him....

Now the snake was the most cunning animal that the Lord God had made. The snake asked the woman, 'Did God really tell you not to eat the fruit from any tree in the garden?'

'We may eat the fruit of any tree in the garden,' the woman answered, 'except the tree in the middle of it. God told us not to eat the fruit of that tree or even touch it; if we do, we will die.'

The snake replied, 'That's not true; you will not die. God said that because he knows that when you eat it you will be like God and know what is good and what is bad.'

The woman saw how beautiful the tree was and how good its fruit would be to eat, and she thought how wonderful it would be to become wise. So she took some of the fruit and ate it. Then she gave some to her husband, and he also ate it. As soon as they had eaten it, they were given understanding and realised that they were naked....

Then the Lord God said to the snake, 'You will be punished for this; you alone of all the animals must bear this curse: from now on you will crawl on your belly, and you will have to eat dust as long as you live. I will make you and the woman hate each other; her offspring and yours will always be enemies. Her offspring will crush your head, and you will bite their heel.'

And he said to the woman, 'I will increase your trouble in pregnancy and your pain in giving birth. In spite of this, you will still have desire for your husband, yet you will be subject to him.'

And he said to the man, 'You listened to your wife and ate the fruit which I told you not to eat. Because of what you have done, the ground will be under a curse. You will have to work hard all your life to make it produce enough food for you. It will produce weeds and thorns, and you will have to eat wild plants. You will have to work hard and sweat to make the soil produce anything, until you go back to the soil from which you were formed. You were made from soil, and you will become soil again.'

Excerpts from the Book of Genesis: chapters 2 and 3 *(Good News Bible)*.

This helps us to see why this style of life was so acceptable to these people and how they were able to sustain themselves in these conditions —

Picture 8
The Snake Charmer by Henri Rousseau (Picture by courtesy of Giraudon)

because of their faith. It gives us an insight into a particular expression of Christianity, its value and its function, that is, how it gives meaning to people's lives.

It also shows how to understand the Genesis story as a picture of the way things are and why they are like they are. That is, hardship is due to a disruption of the way things should be and an exile must precede a return to the way things should be. In this there is an explanation for the present and a hope for the future. Within this story the Puritan settler lives.

Another strategy to build up this understanding in the pupils is for them to divide up into groups or pairs and to compile questions as if they were interviewing the couple. The teacher can discuss with them what might be appropriate sorts of questions to ask.

MAKING ASSOCIATIONS

How we came to be as we are is the theme linked to *The Snake Charmer* by Henri Rousseau in Picture 8.

The picture may be contrasted with the previous Puritan one just discussed. It should also be looked at in relation to the Genesis story reprinted on p.112.

But initially, on its own, it is an evocative picture, and that is what it is meant to be. So the first question I ask my pupils is 'What does the picture suggest to you?'

The air of mystery and the exotic nature of the picture are two things that impress most. Of course the response does not come in this form but often with comments like 'It is weird', 'It is not real' or even 'It is stupid!' However, when probed further the notion of difference and even of fairy tale comes through. We can then move on to the question of whether the picture is meant to depict things as we see them. Clearly not, but often a connection with tropical lands is voiced. 'It is like South Sea Islands are', was one comment and even 'It is like a paradise', which, of course, it is.

However, the feeling of something sinister in the darkness of the picture, the disguised form of the central figure with the diminutive, piercing eyes, and the presence of the snake qualifies this notion. This leads us to a detailed description of what the picture contains which serves to confirm the twin notions of exotic or paradisical and the unknown or sinister which the picture holds in tension. In what then do these twin themes reside? I ask the question, 'Pick on a feature (something) in the picture that is especially productive of the feeling that it conveys to you.' There are a number of responses to this but the most popular emphasise the dominance of the central figure who comes across as female but evil and the vegetation which is somehow larger and more impressive than it ought to be.

Now I ask them to consider this picture and the Genesis passage together. Can they be matched? This is not to say they were ever meant to be but that the motifs in the picture and the motifs in the story are related. This is not surprising when we consider that the picture was painted within a culture that has built its mythological awareness largely out of the Judeo-Christian scriptures, and that there are very strong connections in the myths of religious traditions between the notions of paradise, evil, creation and so forth that often, but not always, share the same symbolism. And this is our task, to attempt to understand the Christian inheritance of our own civilisation.

The pupils often spot the correspondence of evil coming into paradise in the biblical story, and the dark central figure in the picture. I discourage them from trying to make literal associations such as the dark figure is the devil because this is neither necessary nor helpful. What I do ask them to do is feel the effect of the change of the human condition that occurs in the story and in the picture: of course the central dark figure is the key to this. So, despite the picture appearing very static, it expresses a moment of intense dynamism. One student has actually said 'Nothing's happening but something's happening' in the picture. In other words, though there appears to be no action in the picture something appears to be changing in it.

I would contend that we are now more able, through a study of the picture in association with the passage, to draw out one of the central doctrines of the Christian myth of the Fall: that evil entered the world. As a bald statement to a pupil this means nothing, but as conveyed in the picture he can conjure up a feeling related to his own experience. This makes real to him the meaning of the myth. We can then go on to build on this feeling by further questions and classroom activity, such as, 'The figure in the picture has what appears to be a sort of flute in her mouth, what sort of music do you think she is playing.' Pupils may even bring in examples of the sort of music from home. In this way we start to create the mood of the picture in our world of the classroom. This transformation is what both the picture and the myth are about.

Another stimulating question to ask is how they would colour the picture. The central figure often stays black whilst the world around it is very brightly adorned.

A further interesting question is 'Would you like to live there, if there were such a place as this?' Most answer no, some say yes but without the figure and the snakes. However, there is a general feeling of disbelief that such a world exists in actuality, which brings us back to the idea of symbolic representation in both picture and story: we understand something important is being said about ourselves and our world but it is not just a picture of how it looks, or a recounting of historical events.

COMPLETING THE PICTURE

All this has prepared us for the passage below taken from *Pilgrim's Progress* by John Bunyan, and the accompanying picture by Salvador Dali:

As I walked through the wilderness of this world I came to a certain place where there was a den and I lay down to sleep; and as I slept I dreamed a dream. I dreamed I saw a man clothed with rags, standing in a certain place, facing away from his own house, a book in his hand and a great burden on his back. I looked and saw him open the book and read. And, as he read, he wept and trembled. Unable to contain himself he uttered a lamentable cry, saying, 'What shall I do?'

I saw also that he looked this way and that, as if he would run; yet he stood

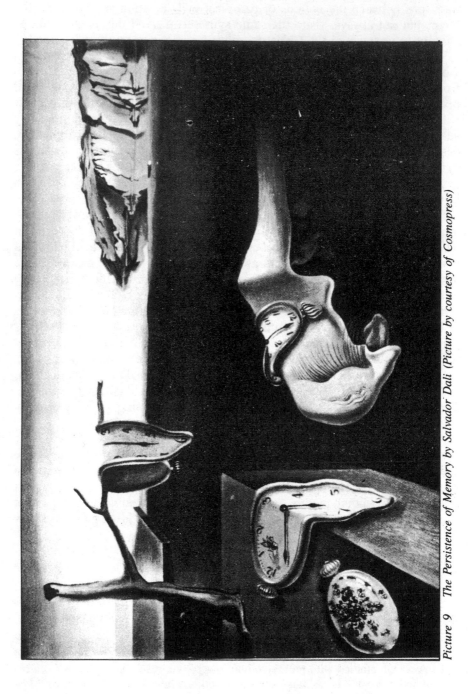

Picture 9   The Persistence of Memory by Salvador Dali (Picture by courtesy of Cosmopress)

still, because he could not tell which way to go. I looked then and saw a man, named Evangelist, coming toward him, who asked:

'Why do you cry?'

He answered: 'Sir, I see from the book in my hand that I am condemned to die, and after that to come to judgement. And I find that I am not willing to do the first, nor able to do the second.'

Then said Evangelist: 'Why not willing to die, since this life is full of so many evils?'

The man answered: 'Because I fear that this burden that is upon my back will sink me lower than the grave.'

Then said Evangelist: 'If this is your condition why do you stand still?' He answered: 'Because I don't know where to go.' Then he gave him a parchment roll and on it was written: 'Fly from the wrath to come.' So I saw in my dream that the man began to run, crying, 'Life, life, eternal life.' He looked not behind him but fled towards the middle of the plain.

The motif that helps us over the bridge from literal to symbolic representation here is dreams. In dreams we enter a world that does not obey the physical laws of time, space and causality of our everyday world, we can accept that 'weird things happen' by acknowledging that dreams are like that. But we are also aware that dreams are related to our everyday life: people we know crop up in them, past events reappear, and, most importantly, dreams reveal our fears, insecurities and anxieties because they are often based on worries, of a coming interview or examination, for example.

Dali's picture can visually draw out the anxiety *(Angst)* of the man in the story through its dreamlike qualities. There is a quality of 'lostness' in the picture as there is in the passage. When the pupils are asked to 'step into the picture and tell me what it is like' this is often referred to. What, then, is missing here that characterises our everyday world? The same element that is missing in our more nightmarish dreams. This is brought out by questions like 'Now you are in the picture in which direction will you go?' The answer is largely 'I don't know' because 'What is the point of going in any direction since I don't know what lies there?'; also, 'There are no familiar landmarks to establish where I am, so how do I know where to go?' Indeed, this is just the problem of Bunyan's traveller. His needs, in relation to his attempts to establish a sense of identity and purpose, are not met by the world he is in. But of course his world is our world, in a psychological sense.

In both cases alienation is the key theme. Understood as 'lostness' this can be related then to experiences pupils have had of feeling lost and how this feeling came about. Naturally the experiences they respond with are expressed in concrete terms of being somewhere unfamiliar but the crucial incident is often the momentary disappearance of a parent, the one who gave meaning to their presence in a certain place. As long as the parent was there they could understand why they were there. When the parent disappeared so did the sense of belonging. The picture with its warped time, represented by the clocks; the landscape without an horizon as sea and sky merge; its utter stillness, etc., convey the same feeling. The passage explains the reason for it, in Christian terms.

Both passage and picture link back to the previous work for further explanation. For example, the guilt in Bunyan's passage is explained only in the light of the Genesis story of the Fall, as is the 'hero's' lack of understanding of where he should go and what he should do.

I now contrast the Rousseau picture and the Dali landscape and ask the pupils to compare them as though the former had been transformed into the latter, with the question, 'What has happened?'

It is obvious that I am using the art to serve my own ends in examining the mythology of Christianity, but I would contend that this is perfectly legitimate since I am not imposing a normative interpretation on the pictures in question but showing how their themes and motifs can help to explain connected ideas in Christianity. That does not dictate the interpretation of the art as 'Christian'. It does not distort the intention of the artist in any way. It is necessary to have some understanding of the pictures used and how visual material can be appreciated and explored. This does not demand specialised skills of the teacher, but only the use of simple techniques.

The way in which I have explored the use of these pictures and passages is not the only way they may be used, though certain connections, I hope, were obvious. But this method is meant as an exploration for pupils and teachers alike. There is no strictly didactic aim involved in teaching from these resources, simply the development of the skills necessary to spot associations and build up a particular awareness of how human experience can be understood within Christian terms.

NOTE

These resources have been used in the Chichester Project textbook '*Christian Experience*', which I produced, with accompanying questions and suggestions.

16 Visits to Christian places of worship

Cherry Gould

WHY SHOULD VISITS FORM PART OF RELIGIOUS EDUCATION?

Visits to places of worship are one of the most accessible ways open to Religious Education of making a religion come alive. Slides, filmstrips and videos are a tremendous asset but must always, by their very nature, be secondhand experiences. Visits provide the opportunity to see things at first-hand. They encourage pupils to use all of their senses. More important is the feeling that the atmosphere of the building is sometimes able to convey. It is the experience of visiting a place of worship that can occasionally enable pupils to catch a glimpse of what a believer feels.

VARIOUS AIMS

One aim of visits is to allow pupils to see for real things that they have only discussed and seen pictures of in the classroom. Visits provide a way of becoming familiar with the 'furniture' and the layout of the building. Secondary pupils ought to be able to distinguish the interior of a Catholic church from that of, say, a Baptist church. They ought to be able to see what theological statements are made by the 'furniture' and its position within the building. It is important that they should begin to see the diversity of church buildings and the uses to which they are put. Churches can be a resource for work done as part of a local history project where pupils might look at the marriage or baptismal registers, or at the graveyard.

FEELING COMFORTABLE IN CHURCHES

Another aim of making visits is to enable pupils to feel comfortable in churches and familiarise them with what happens inside. I have known non-church-going adults who have found the prospect of going into an unfamiliar church a daunting experience. A large number of rites of passage in Britain still occur in churches. It is vital that Religious Education should equip young people to understand what happens inside churches. They should know how to conduct themselves within these buildings; be able to recognise what they see inside; and, not least, they should grow to feel at ease there. It is a fact that fewer and fewer children are familiar with churches on a regular, or even on an occasional basis, such as is provided by baptism or wedding services. I have been surprised at the number of children for whom their school church visit has been their first time inside any church. This unfamiliarity can have dire consequences. On one visit to a parish church I found a small group using the altar as a table for writing up their notes. They did not intend to be disrespectful but simply had no idea that this would have offended some of the parishioners.

ENCOUNTERING PREJUDICE

Some aims are tied to particular localities. Whilst I was teaching in west Cumbria, an area sometimes described as a miniature Northern Ireland, there was a lot of latent hostility in the community amongst the nominal Christians, which manifested itself in the schools. This, it is important to note, was non-existent amongst the majority of practising Christians who displayed tremendous ecumenical goodwill.

On several occasions, prior to class visits, pupils informed me that they did not think they would be allowed to visit the Catholic church. Once a parent complained to the head about my keeping her son in to do homework because it was on the subject of the Catholic church.

However, as far as it is possible to ascertain, this prejudice did seem to diminish following visits to the Catholic church. One pupil took his parents to see how the church had been modernised, after he had made a school visit. On another occasion a lad decided to do his free-choice homework on the Catholic church in his village and knocked on the priest's door to ask for help. The priests were seen as human – and likeable humans at that. One who was a Manchester United fanatic made quite an impression!

THE VARIETY OF CHRISTIAN PLACES OF WORSHIP –
THE CHRISTIAN FAMILY

Even the smallest of towns in Britain has a variety of Christian places of worship which can be visited. West Cumbria may be devoid of gurdwaras, mandirs, mosques and synagogues, but even the smallest of villages has a church and, often, at least one chapel.

It is impossible to take pupils to visit every single type of place used for Christian worship. One has to be selective. At secondary level, I take pupils to visit at least three types of church building – a Catholic and/or Anglican church, a Free church such as Baptist, Methodist, Pentecostal or United Reformed, and a Friends' meeting-house or a Salvation Army citadel.

Despite the variety the teacher must ensure that the pupils recognise all the churches as belonging to the Christian family. Young people seem prone to think of Christianity and some of the Churches, usually the Catholic, as being entirely different religions.

ARRANGING VISITS

When arranging visits it is essential for the teacher to establish personal contact with the church. An initial meeting with the minister or a church representative enables the teacher to explain the purpose of the intended visit and its part in the scheme of work. It also enables the host to know the age and ability of the pupils.

A preliminary visit to the church provides the teacher with an opportunity to familiarise herself, or himself, with the building and to plan the actual class visit. It also enables the drafting of a worksheet. The person who is to be the host at the church often appreciates having a copy of the worksheet beforehand. Finally, I would advise ringing the church the day prior to a visit to check that there are no unforeseen circumstances which will mean postponing the visit. I was sternly chastised by one of my classes for not taking them to a funeral! A colleague who had not followed this procedure had unwittingly done this with another group.

When a relationship between the church and the school is well established, a telephone call a week or so before an intended visit is often sufficient. It is always better to give as much notice as possible if the minister or a church member is asked to be there, or if the building is not normally open during the week. A telephone call the day before the visit is still necessary.

INSIDE THE BUILDING

Inside the building I find it helpful to let the pupils sit quietly first for a few moments. This gives them the opportunity to pause, and perhaps reflect. It may help them to get the 'feel' of the building. Often it also serves to still them and enable them to look around quietly.

If there is a host from the church it is a good idea to introduce them after this period of quiet. I find it helpful for the host to give a brief introduction to the church's main features, emphasising how the church is used for worship, rather than recounting its history. This may then lead to questions from the group.

After this the class can look around the building; sometimes this will mean breaking up into smaller groups. The host may be able to show the group particular items of interest such as the vestry, the vestments, the chapels of reconciliation or confessionals, the organ, the belfry, and the room used for Sunday school or meetings, etc.

An opportunity should be given for pupils to look around on their own and to study more closely what interests them.

I think it is important to bring all the group back together again after they have looked round individually or been working in smaller groups. It provides a good opportunity to ask any final questions, thank the host and, perhaps, pause for a moment's silence before departing.

This basic format could be used with children of all ages, though obviously the content will vary depending on the age of the children. A priest may simulate an infant baptism using a doll to show younger children what happens at this service.

I have considered church visits primarily as a means of looking at a building used for worship. However, a visit could form part of a local history project. Emphasis could be placed on looking at baptismal and marriage registers, memorials in the church, tombstones in the graveyard and, where appropriate, making brass rubbings.

WORKSHEETS?

It is helpful for pupils to be equipped with a pen, a pencil, a piece of paper and a clipboard before leaving school on a visit. The clipboard need not be a grand affair, as a simple home made one can be achieved with a strong piece of cardboard and a peg. It will give the pupils something other than pews to rest on.

How useful are worksheets, especially if we are trying to encourage the pupils to use all their senses and to see the visit on a level other than the purely factual? They can help focus pupils' minds and direct their attention. They can serve as an aid for writing up notes for homework, or in a class next lesson. They give the impression to our hosts and to any worshippers present that this is part of a scheme that will be followed up rather than a jaunt out. They can be useful in preparing visits with hosts, many of whom like to see them beforehand. After several visits the teacher can compile a revised worksheet from her or his previous experience. Questions asking what features pupils find most beautiful and most surprising, how they feel upon entering, and how they think a worshipper might feel upon entering, can elicit other than merely factual responses. Giving pupils a long set of questions and then asking them to pick, say, six or seven to answer is a method I have often used. I have also always included a question asking pupils to note down anything they have not had an opportunity to record elsewhere. On some occasions I have simply discarded the worksheet altogether because it was obvious that it would be a barrier to real learning. On these occasions the flow of dialogue between the pupils and their host was such that it was not right to interrupt it. Choosing the moment to give out the worksheets is vitally important. If the pupils have them before entering the building some tend to be more eager to fill it out than listen to what the host is saying. It can be useful, even on a meagre one lesson a week, to spend fifteen minutes of the lesson prior to the visit going through it, so that pupils have already read it through and know what they are expected to do.

WHAT A BUILDING IS SAYING THEOLOGICALLY

Secondary age pupils should be able to begin to work out what the building is saying theologically. They should see what the position of a piece of furniture says about its function for the worshippers in that particular church. In a Catholic or Anglican church the fact that the altar is in the centre will emphasise the centrality of the Mass or Eucharist in the worship. In a Free church, such as a Baptist or Pentecostalist building, the fact that the pulpit is in the centre will disclose the centrality of preaching the Word. It is important to remember that there will always be variations and exceptions to the rule!

The absence of a font in Baptist or Pentecostalist buildings should alert pupils to the fact that, in some churches, babies are not baptised. They should be ready and on the look-out for a baptistry and aware of its significance regarding believers' baptism. This is always a point of interest with children who, in my experience, usually grasp this theological point quite readily.

In a Salvation Army citadel or a Friends' meeting-house, pupils should be aware of why no font, baptistry, altar, or communion table is found. They should recognise the importance of the Salvationist flag in the citadel under which new soldiers are sworn in.

The absence of any furniture other than seats in a circle in a Quaker meeting-house should help them to see what theological point Quakers are making when they speak of 'the priesthood of all believers'.

The way worshippers of different Christian traditions regard their place of worship should become apparent to even the youngest of children as they enter the building. They will sense an aura of holiness in a Catholic church when Catholics make the sign of the cross with water from the stoup as they enter the church and genuflect when passing the Tabernacle. They will get a different perspective when they visit a Baptist or Salvation Army place of worship which is altogether plainer and where the rooms used for worship are often multi-purpose. The room where worship will take place on Sundays could be the lunch club for senior citizens in the week.

PREPARATION AND FOLLOW-UP WORK

Visits to churches will clearly take place within a part of the syllabus devoted to Christianity or within relevant topic work. Since more than a visit to one church may well be planned, follow-up work may also be preparation for what comes next. A checklist of what you are hoping pupils will observe, related to the worksheet you may use, can form the basis for discussion, reflection and group work. This must highlight the variety of different types of buildings and furnishings, pointing to the various emphases of different Christian denominations whilst also recognising what they have in common. It must also allow for the pupils to make a response to the effect the visit had on them.

The web diagram (Picture 10) indicates some possibilities for the teacher and is one way of presenting the pupils with an observation exercise, whilst visiting churches, which can provide the data for follow-up work.

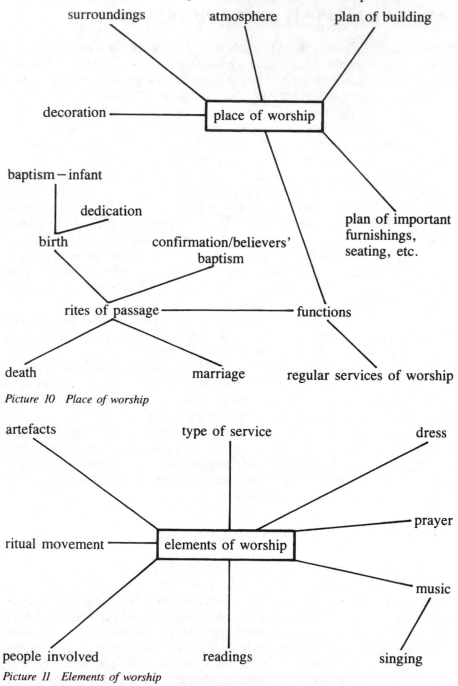

Picture 10   Place of worship

Picture 11   Elements of worship

The pupils can be encouraged to fill this in with more detail which will then produce a record on which they can base their comments regarding similarities and differences.

A similar task such as that in Picture 11 could also be used if an actual service is attended.

How far the teacher goes in filling in these diagrams as a preparation and aid to the pupils will depend on the particular group involved. With some groups the detail that can be included makes the final result quite complex and leads on to theological questions.

More penetrating questions can also be asked, such as: 'When and how do people talk to God in the service?' and 'When and how is God thought to be talking to them?'.

In the follow-up work in class it is important to maintain the visual impact of the visit both for stimulus and recall. This can either be done with slides or pictures of various features of a church's altar, pulpit, lectern, aisle, seating, etc. or by having slide pictures taken of the church actually visited, which is far better, of course.

This can be done in advance or involve the pupils by asking them what they would take pictures of as a record of their visit.

Additional ideas on this topic related to four − eight year olds but useful for older children can be found in the Hampshire Handbook *Paths to Understanding*, pp.26−9.

After a visit it is important to see that thanks are given to the host. Thank-you letters are an important exercise for pupils maintaining a good relationship with the places visited.

DRAWBACKS − FORTY MINUTES

Primary teachers will have fewer problems in arranging visits as regards time than will their colleagues in secondary schools.

Trying to arrange a visit with only one period of forty minutes, which is still all many secondary schools have, is almost impossible. I combated this by visiting places which were literally on the doorstep. Then, after consultation with the head, I bargained with colleagues whose lesson with the class preceded or followed mine. This seemed to underline the case for more time for RE in the following year! Asking for a double RE lesson, so as not to cause disruption to colleagues when arranging visits, may prove a good timetable tactic!

AN RE FIELD DAY

Places that are too far to be visited within a lesson can sometimes be visited on an RE field day. I run such a field day for all second years in the summer term. On this trip we usually visit a cathedral, a Baptist church, a Friends' meeting-house and, when possible, an Anglican church whose 'furniture' has been altered to suit the worship. The advantage of such a day trip was that places further afield could be visited quite cheaply (it usually cost pupils under

£2) and it was seen as a good day out. The lunch hour spent in a park playing crazy golf or football seemed to be a great attraction! Over a couple of years a trip like this can become an expected annual school journey and an integral part of the syllabus. It can be possible to get 99, if not 100 per cent, attendance. At one of my schools where Jehovah's Witness children had been withdrawn from RE they came and asked to go on the visit. Enjoyment promotes interest!

SIX HOURS OF SOMEONE'S TIME... ONLY PRIESTS AND MINISTERS ARE RELIGIOUS

Attempting to include all the pupils of a single year group in even a moderately- sized school puts tremendous demands on the church to be visited if someone is expected to greet each group. If six classes visit one church and are able to spend an hour there, you are asking for six hours of someone's time. The person most likely to welcome and speak to the pupils is a clergyman. This can present another problem. The pupils could get the impression that only priests and ministers are religious. How many of us have had to encounter the argument: 'Why do I have to do RE when I don't want to be a nun or a vicar?' The impression could also be given that religion is the prerogative of men. Not all hosts, it must be mentioned finally, are good at explaining things to young people. It may be necessary to guide the introduction and the initial questions.

THE CHURCH CANNOT REALLY BE SEEN

A major drawback is, of course, the fact that during the school week the church cannot really be seen. In the middle of the week pupils can only see one, or perhaps two, representatives of the church, and the building where they congregate for worship. The teacher will need to emphasise that churches are not simply buildings. Sometimes groups are fortunate in seeing additional church members besides the host. They may be preparing and serving lunches to senior citizens, engaged in cleaning, or spending time quietly in prayer. In my experience, the churches that tend to be the most well used in the week for prayers are Roman Catholic but then, by and large, they are the ones which have been able to stay open during the week.

THE LIVING CHURCH

The class can be encouraged to think about the church from the point of view of its members by looking at the church noticeboard and finding out about its concerns and activities. The best way of ensuring that pupils see the living church is to take them to a service on Sunday. This, of course, can only be done on a voluntary basis but I have found no shortage of eager volunteers to see what various services are like.

VISITS CONVEY THE SENSE OF THE RELIGION

The most important reason in my opinion for making visits to churches an integral part of the work on Christianity is that they convey the sense of the religion in a way that nothing else can. It is the deeper feeling that often only visits can convey. A small row of flickering candles can speak to some pupils in a way no words can. A Quaker meeting-house may not be regarded as 'holy' by Quakers. However, I have seen classes fall naturally quiet upon entering the room used by Friends for worship, even though it looked no different from a station or doctor's waiting room.

HOPES

I hope that pupils will come away remembering how human their hosts were. It would be good if they remember the importance of the things they have seen inside, and understood what is happening around them if they enter churches later in their life. I hope they will be able to feel comfortable and at ease. I was delighted to read a comment in a third year girl's letter to the United Reformed minister after our visit: 'I feel I may drop in again.' Whatever their own beliefs or stance I hope visits will encourage pupils to be open and tolerant towards the beliefs of others. Above all, I hope that they have been able to glimpse that sense of 'the other' so that they can truly understand what it might mean to take Christianity seriously.

17 Teaching about belief: trust and risk

David Morling

Christianity is such a familiar background to the lives of so many people in our society that there is rarely any consideration given to the thinking that might lie behind people's responses to this faith. Some people assume you can simply inherit faith. Other people assume that provable facts lie behind all our important knowledge of the world. It is thought that we either gather information empirically, or from some other person who has gathered it empirically. Thus information from science is readily accepted but when it is found that religion cannot be considered on this basis it is often rejected as having no truth.

If pupils are to appreciate Christianity it is necessary for them to understand the nature of religious belief, and the possibility that it might be a reasoned reaction to the ideas of one's society and personal feelings, in the same way as we come to hold other beliefs about ourselves and the world around us. This will help pupils to understand why it is that some people find it reasonable to commit their lives to living as members of a faith like Christianity.

AIMS

The central aim of this course of lessons is to develop an understanding of the complexity of human response to religion and to Christianity, in particular, and it is for this purpose that it has been incorporated into our school's Religious Education programme in the fourth year. While there is misunderstanding about belief within human thinking, pupils will find it difficult to understand why people have a religious faith at all. To explain this we set the following aims:

1. to give some fuller meaning to the word 'belief' and show that it is an

important aspect of our everyday decision-making about the world;

2. to show that belief is a basis for action;

3. to show a need to appreciate what faith is, through understanding the words we use;

4. to consider the complexity of decisions of faith made up, as they are, of reasoning plus risk;

5. to show that there is a similarity between decisions of faith and other areas of human discernment.

THE WHOLE COURSE

We develop these lessons over about ten hours which, for us, represents about half a term. There is no shortage of material and the difficulty lies rather in keeping within this allotted time since the pupils tend to take full advantage of the opportunity for discussion. It is important that there is discussion because the work is based upon the idea that the teacher is guiding, yet sharing in, an exploration of this complex business of understanding the way we think. *The course contains the following elements*:

1. an exercise to distinguish facts, opinions and the frequent uncertainties in deciding about truth, for example, by deciding the truth content of some simple statements and comparing results within the group;

2. an exercise to examine how we decide when things are true, for example, by pupils working in groups and preparing, and then demonstrating the truth of certain things to their fellows;

3. an examination of the types of evidence people will accept as a basis for decision and action, for example, by describing things as if experienced by a Martian visitor, to show the complex information on which we depend for understanding;

4. an examination of belief from feelings, for example, by using a passage from literature which describes a character's sense of there being an unseen presence, as in some of the passages in William Golding's *Lord of the Flies*;

5. an examination of belief in action, showing its elements of trust and risk and the commitment of individuals, by using one or more biographies of believers.

BELIEF IN ACTION – TRUST AND RISK

We will concentrate here on just one part of the course: that concerned with living through belief despite the uncertainties that this involves. The general assumption seems to be that Christianity in particular, and religion in general, is exceptional in having these elements of trust and risk. We therefore introduce, at this point, people who have committed their lives to a cause or overriding aim, to show that any life-commitment is not dissimilar to religious belief. Since pupils have a great respect for the achievements of science, the work of a scientist provides a valuable approach to this. In many ways the adventure of doing science is similar to the adventure of being involved in a religion.

We begin this section with the story of Marie and Pierre Curie, whose work, at the end of the nineteenth century, demonstrated the existence of radium. They committed their lives to an idea and there followed a long period of uncertainty and hard work before they were able to find confirmation of what they believed to be true. Other scientists' work could be examined in a similar way, such as the slow formation of Darwin's ideas, or the struggle Watt had to establish his.

Pupil work

Using a young person's biography of Marie and Pierre Curie (because it covers a lot of ground in a very few pages) we offer the story to the pupils to read. Following this, pupils are given time, in small groups, to prepare answers to some questions.

(a) In order to establish that pupils have grasped what Marie and Pierre were doing:

1. What were the Curies trying to do?

(b) In order to establish the existence of risk, according to the pupils' understanding of the nature of risk:

2. With hindsight, were there any unknown risks?

3. Were there any known risks?

(c) In order to introduce consideration of why the Curies should have attempted the task at all:

4. Was it exciting work?

5. Did it produce exciting results?

6. What made them think it was worth doing?

Pupils are instructed that examples and reasons are required for each answer. Each pupil is asked to answer the following questions individually during this same session:

A. What risks have you taken in the past?

B. What risks are you likely to take in the future?

Only about half an hour is allowed for these tasks and regular promptings are given to keep the pupils moving through them. A basic response over all the questions is more important than answers in depth. It is hoped that the depth comes in the class discussions that follow.

Reporting pupil responses

The discussions reported in some of the following sections could not all take place in the actual time allowed for these exercises. The points raised here are derived from teaching this material over a number of years and on any one occasion the discussions can take a number of directions. The teacher has to judge the most pressing issues for a particular class and allow the discussions to develop accordingly. The assumption of this work is that pupils do make false relationships between belief, truth and human motivation. In talking about these things the teacher does not have to impose a view, rather, the pupils will find, by their own comments and examples, a more adequate description of things.

Pupil responses

These questions are directly related to the sort of comments that pupils make about being involved with religious belief. There will always be comments on the lack of interest they experience from involvement with religion, by which they mean Christianity.

Question 1* is simply there to ensure that attention has been paid to the text and almost all pupils note that the Curies were trying to prove the existence of radium. *Questions 2 and 3* are more important. Pupils note the unknown risk of radiation poisoning and the known risk that they may have found that radium didn't exist at all, which would have meant that their work would have been wasted. There is a problem here, because while all science is built on the fact that experiments can bring results which falsify the theory being tested, this is not true of science as it is conducted in the school laboratory. Therefore the pupils' experience of science does not usually include the excitement of uncertainty. Whatever happens in their experiments, there is always a right answer known by the teacher. We have found it very helpful to discuss this matter with our science colleagues in the school to see how they come to terms with this. Fortunately, some pupils do see the point that you do not always get the information that you expected. Discussion can be opened up on the value of experiments that produce unexpected answers and, most important of all, on the fact that scientists act on the basis of their theories, which always contain an element of uncertainty, and which can never be deemed fully proven. Some pupils will respond with incredulity, 'All that work and they don't know how it's going to work out. I wouldn't bother.' However, there are always those who have been in some sort of outdoor activity like sailing, caving or rock climbing who will say that it is the element of risk that makes it worthwhile. Sometimes this may come from those who argue the same point of view from having indulged in illegal or anti-social activities!

Another area that we often get into is that even answers which disprove theories are useful, that all knowledge is important even when it includes something that we did not expect to find. The most common way that this appears is when they speak of 'that bloke that found penicillin; he didn't expect it, did he?'. A good source of additional material to have at hand for this discussion is the 'This Week' and 'Science' sections of the *New Scientist* magazine.

Questions 4–6 relate to the value of a task in relation to the process by which it is achieved. Often the pupils speak as if they are concerned only about the value of the task. 'No, it was no good, it was boring,' is perhaps one of the most common comments. In response to the lives of the Curies, about two-thirds will say it was exciting work, even though the biographies make it clear that the actual work was tedious and repetitive. However, additional comments in written answers and discussions make it clear that

*For the wording of the questions refer back to p.130

the pupils do recognise the tedium of the actual task. There is a tendency to mix up answers to Questions 4 and 5. Pupils will talk of the fact that the work brought them fame or the pleasure of being the first. A telling comment was: 'The Curies thought it was important so that it was exciting to them.' This created useful thoughts in relation to the pupils' own experiences of studying for examinations. A very sensitive response on one occasion was, 'I don't know. They discovered a lot but there was a lot of pain on the way.'

A less constructive response is that the Curies did all this because they were in some way peculiar. 'They were fanatics', or 'They liked discovering things, they were that sort of people'. This is a common response made towards pupils who make special efforts and may well be a defence against the need to decide to be responsible for oneself. There is often a similar response to people who are very successful at school. We need to consider it, because when applied to religious experience it can become, 'It's all very well for Jesus, he was different, but it's got nothing to do with me.' This needs discussion upon the nature of outstanding people and whether they are in fact odd. Pupils may offer biographies of sporting or entertainment personalities where there is usually an emphasis upon the way that they are ordinary folk who made particular efforts. In the case of the Curies this can be seen through a brief review of their family life and leisure pursuits.

It is important to note that *Questions A and B* (see p.139) have already been answered in writing before any discussion has taken place so they are likely to colour that discussion throughout. However, they do need individual consideration. Pupils like talking about past risks they have taken, and possible answers are numerous: the cheeky ones – coming to school, having not done their homework; the adventurous ones – parascending, or climbing: the educational ones – working for exams, working for D of E Awards; and the rebellious ones – riding a motorbike illegally, or cheeking a teacher. The important thing is that all the pupils show that they have taken decisions, often important ones, where the outcomes are uncertain.

As for 'risks of the future', marriage is most commonly given as an answer. Other fairly frequent answers include things like the choice of a career, driving, becoming a parent or getting involved in a sport. Pupils generally refer to the fact that one can become physically or emotionally hurt in these situations, and there are anecdotes of how people that they know have been. They also show a sense of uncertainty where they are involved with objects, other people or complex events over which they cannot exercise control. The pupils show that they realise that they cannot be sure of their own conduct in the future.

All the answers to these two questions allow a more fundamental problem to be presented to the class. Why do we do things which have an element of risk? If marriage is risky, why do people get married? Discussion leading from this clearly shows that pupils appreciate that risk is a part of life. We do often act without proof or certainty but that does not mean we act without sense or reason. Pupils point to the influence and example of other people, which suggests that despite the risks, there is something worthwhile at the end. The discussion also often arrives at comments which suggest that the more important the thing is, the more it seems worth taking the risk. These points seem to arise most easily when the discussion is centred upon marriage as an example.

THE LINKED SESSION OF PUPIL WORK

The following lesson is devoted explicitly to Christian belief. Pupils are told that we are to explore the same issues of risk in relation to taking decisions about religion.

Consideration of the work of Marie and Pierre Curie suggests that our ideas about the world are tested by the things we do. Furthermore, that we have to commit ourselves without any guarantee of the outcome. It is not that certain types of decisions in life bring risk, but that all life decisions involve risk. Thus we can examine the way that some people have taken decisions about religion and relate them to the way we generally take decisions about our lives.

Examples from the New Testament may make a useful starting point:
Matthew 4:18−22   The call of the disciples
John 20:26−29   Thomas' response to the risen Christ
Acts 9:1−9 and 17−19.   Paul's conversion

These three stories all offer an example of a moment of decision yet they provide a variety of circumstances within which the decisions were made. The disciples are challenged to a radical change of life by a face-to-face meeting. Thomas makes a decision within the progress of his commitment to Jesus. Paul is already heavily committed, in religious terms, and he is called on to change direction (His actual experience is also different and we might consider whether we would think of it as visionary or internal.) In all these cases it is important that the content of these events be considered, especially to show that individual decisions are embedded within a succession of decisions which are constantly necessary in living life, and therefore in living a religious commitment in Christian terms.

Pupils are asked to respond to these biblical stories with two sets of questions:
1. Why do you think that the characters in the biblical stories behaved as they did? What do you think of their decisions?
2. What do you think of people accepting the risk of Christianity as the basis of their lives? Why do you think they do it?

Again a limited amount of time is allowed for written work so that they have just a basic starting-point for the discussion that will follow.

Pupil responses

It is clear that doubting Thomas' reactions are the ones that make most sense to a lot of pupils. 'I think Thomas was right to disbelieve until he had felt the wounds.' This relates to frequent comments like, 'I couldn't believe in someone who I've never seen and there isn't any proof that he exists.' This brings us back to the basic matter of this course and the nature of what is sufficient to allow a person to believe and act on that belief. One pupil even interpreted Paul's conversion in that way.

> Saul did not believe in God because he had never actually heard or seen God so why should he believe, then when he heard God he believed it because God had made him blind, to prove that he was actually there alive.

It was valuable to relate this comment to the way that pupils might feel if they had a similar experience. What response would it evoke in them?

Even more egocentric are those responses which suggest that there is no truth to be concerned about, that we need do only what we feel like doing. 'I'm naturally lazy, so I don't think I would bother,' or the comment, 'I expect being a fisherman was boring so it was a change.' These responses remind us that pupils will judge the behaviour of others against the yardstick of their own motives. It is a common type of response in class discussion. It implies the need for other discussions on our individuality and the influences of the world around us.

Another set of responses suggests that it was all right in those days but that things have changed and it's much more difficult now. 'If I was alive in Jesus' day I would follow him and become one of his followers,' may be contrasted with comments relating to today like, 'It was OK then, but people today would call you some kind of nutter.' Perhaps there is in this last comment evidence of the desire to limit the challenge of Christianity to what may be conveniently carried out by people today. 'I would base some of what I do on the teaching of Jesus but I would not go to the extremes of the example above.' Discussion can be directed at this point to what sort of commitment is reasonable and what sort of efforts they would be willing to make.

This leads us on to a discussion about why it might be uncomfortable to be a Christian now. That is, what is the discomfort that might arise as a result of taking that risk? 'Taking Christianity into your lives is risky, there might not even be a God, heaven, etc. You get the mickey taken. You have to give money to the Church.' Here it is suggested that the outcome is uncertain and the process uncomfortable, so why worry? What they have done is to ignore the possible outcomes. Again the link is not being made with the way we take similar decisions elsewhere in life. 'Basing your life on Christianity might upset your life to an extent where it would become unbearably strict.' The problem with such answers in terms of religious understanding is that they show a failure to grasp what is meant by religious commitment, despite the work that they have done at school or their experiences elsewhere. The fact is that social attitudes have a more powerful effect upon the thinking of pupils than the carefully built and presented ideas that we try to teach.

The ability to disconnect religion and life may be implied. 'I don't think Christianity is a big risk unless you are going to be a monk or a nun and spend all your life with God.' This opens up a vital area of discussion about the relationship between religion and life. 'If anyone asked me if it was worth being a Christian, I would probably say "no", because it is easy to put in an appearance at church and look holy but it is not so easy in everyday life to do God's work.' This reveals a problem with the Christian Church throughout its history where daily actions have been at variance with vision. It is one of the greatest problems of all for pupils to appreciate the Church as a society of redeemed sinners; they see it, rather, as a failed community who have claimed sainthood.

There is often a difference of opinion in discussion as to whether Christianity is the norm or the exception in our society. A pupil's point of view on this largely depends upon whether they equate society with their own contemporaries, which would suggest Christianity is the exception, or think of adult society, where they seem to assume it is the norm. 'If you live with dropouts Christianity is a great risk. If you live in a normal society quite a lot of Christians will be normal anyway.' 'We have been brought up to believe and worship Him because it is the dominant religion among our community. It would be anti-social to become anti-Christ.' These comments bring their contradictions, 'You may lose a lot of friends because they think you are a religious twit. I do not think it is very good to make Christianity a basis of our lives because it does not fit in with our society.'

Often there are Christian pupils who possess a direct simple faith. They often keep out of the discussion although they are very clear in their written answers. 'I think it's the best risk I've ever taken when I asked God into my life and I know it's a hard path to follow, but I manage it and have much joy in it.' Such answers suggest a faith based on a personal experience, where the argument is, 'If you had experienced what I have experienced you would believe in it too.' Such assurance is powerful for that individual but it brings derision when it is argued within the general discussion. However, the feelings of these pupils also have to be considered as the discussion develops. It is important to try and get these pupils to communicate their experience in an open way.

THE VALUE OF THE WORK

In our experience these discussions have been both exciting, as we probe some of these basic issues, and depressing, as pupils go back to defensive comments which avoid the challenge of these issues. This suggests that while a course like this does confront difficult areas and make some impact, it does not solve all problems of understanding, and we have to accept that many uncertainties remain. Often it is found that discussions do more to write the agenda for future lessons than to give a feeling of progress made in the present.

As the opening paragraphs suggest, the course attempts to correct assumptions common in our society, so that the teacher must not expect an obvious and dramatic change in the way that pupils think. However, coupled with the fact that these issues are implicit elsewhere in the Religious Education syllabus, a greater sensitivity can be developed in this important area of understanding if pupils are only given the opportunity to appreciate *why* people hold religious faith.

BOOKS RECOMMENDED FOR FURTHER READING

The following three books introduce the issues of the nature of belief, religion and experience, as they are considered in contemporary debate.

MacLaren, E. (1979) *The Nature of Belief*, London, Sheldon Press.
Donovan, P. (1979) *Interpreting Religious Experience*, London, Sheldon Press.
Küng, H. (1978) *On Being a Christian*, London, Collins. (Esp. sections D.I. and II, pp.511–53). Presents a vigorous exposition of the place of faith in the life of a twentieth-century human being.

In order to present the work on Marie and Pierre Curie the teacher might find it useful to read:
Curie, E. (1976) *Madame Curie*, London, Heinemann.

While for their pupils a young person's biography would be needed, such as:
Birch, B. (1982) *Marie Curie*, London, MacDonald Educational.

Other useful stimulus material for teachers from which excerpts for pupils can be selected include:
Bronowski, J. (1973) *The Ascent of Man*, London, BBC (see esp. Chapter II–'Knowledge or Certainty').
Golding, W. (1954) *Lord of the Flies*, London, Faber (see esp. Chapter 7–'Shadows and tall trees').
Dimitriu, P. (1983) *Incognito*, London, Sphere, pp.350–56.
Matthew Arnold's poem 'Dover Beach'.

18 Teaching about Jesus: an upper school experience

Harry Stephens

THE CONTEXT

I teach in a comprehensive upper school of about 1000 students. In its intake year (the third year of secondary school) all pupils have two lessons of Religious Studies per week. This provides one and a half hours contact time plus a homework slot. As part of that year's curriculum about eighteen lessons are spent on a 'Jesus' theme entitled 'Jesus the puzzle'. This theme does not represent the only work pupils will have done about Jesus, nor, if they opt for examination work, will it be their last. In effect, this Jesus topic is to be understood as an evaluative and exploratory exercise. It serves both as a climax of and a reflection upon past work in first and middle schools. All intake year Religious Studies is taught in mixed-ability groups.

JESUS THE PUZZLE – THE SCHEME

Here are outlined the various parts of the scheme. Objectives are shown in italics with suggestions of how they may be achieved shown under the heading of 'Method'.

Introduction

To stimulate interest in the question 'Who is or was Jesus?'

Method

This single 'impact' lesson uses a homemade slide/tape sequence mixing music and visual images of Jesus, and reflecting the variety of ways in which western culture presents Jesus. Stills from *Jesus of Nazareth*, slides from the CEM pack *Christ in Art* and music such as *Jesus Christ Superstar*, *Godspell* and *The Messiah* provide some of the material for this.

Describing a person/describing Jesus

To show that there is no one agreed descripton of Jesus; and that sources of information about Jesus need investigation and evaluation

Method

Pupils are asked to suggest questions they could ask of another person to get 'a helpful picture in their minds' of an absent person, whom only the questioned person knows. These same questions are then asked about Jesus. In small groups, pupils give answers to each question, including 'How do you know?' (i.e. sources of information). The answers to some of these questions are tabulated for each group on the OHP or board for all to see. Discussion then ensues based on issues these answers raise.

Immediately the 'faith' and 'fact' issues will be exposed. There will also be questions relating to how to interpret what pupils have learned in the past. One suspects that Jesus has been presented as a neat package not only by many schools but also by Churches and the media. Here I hope to reveal that this cannot be the case.

This lesson usually gives an indication of those areas of most interest to a class, suggesting that they are worth greater emphasis during the theme.

Jesus in art

The objectives and method are examined in some detail on pp.141–43.

Did Jesus actually exist?

To consider what constitutes good evidence and to encourage open-minded enquiry

Method

A surprising number of pupils of this age doubt that the Jesus of history actually lived.

Pupils are asked to look at a summary of the rather vague, non-Christian early references to Jesus. Their apparent corroboration of some New Testament detail is made clear. Pupils are also told that few serious historians deny the existence of an historical Jesus but that little if anything is known about him outside the Gospel accounts. There is a hope that by these means and the showing of the video film, *The Silent Witness* (about the Turin Shroud), pupils will begin to realise more directly that it is 'faith' questions that most divide people. In other words, the question is not whether he existed, but who he was and what significance his life had. It is this sort of question that is subject to considerable and varied interpretation.

This work draws from chapter 4 of the Chichester Project book, *Jesus*, by Trevor Shannon. The video film is available from Screenpro, London, or various local resource centres.

A man, a message and pupils' reactions

To think imaginatively about some of the ways in which the story and stories of Jesus may have been communicated and enshrined in the early Church community; pupils should be able to use this experience to consider the nature of the Gospel narratives

Method

A 'visitor' enters the classroom and delivers 'the Message' (a secularised paraphrase of Luke 6:27–35). This is then discussed once the 'visitor' leaves. The message is judged and responded to by the pupils. They also consider how such a message could be preserved and passed on efficiently if the 'visitor' had died. The accuracy of oral communication and techniques of memorisation are tried out. The nature of propaganda is considered (often in relation to political propaganda at election times).

Jewish Rabbinic practices may be mentioned. Some of the ways the Gospels have included passages that are arranged for easier memorisation are sometimes detailed (e.g. the Beatitudes and the poetry in St John's Gospel).

They should realise that human experience shows that any 'message' of the sort originating from Jesus will become interwoven with 'the person' of that message. Pupils will be asked to think about how and why a message might become changed. A 'living tradition' is a hard concept to grasp. In this section there is a serious attempt to tackle this and to relate the work to the tradition of the Christian community — the community of faith in Jesus.

Examining the written evidence

To consider carefully the nature and purpose of the Gospels and other early Church writings with particular reference to their liturgical and evangelistic uses

Method

Using a worksheet, pupils have time to discover the main documents and what we know of their origins. This is outline work only — not a detailed biblical study. The work, supplemented with a filmstrip, considers what a

Gospel is and what it is not. The 'faith' purpose and liturgical uses are considered and related to contemporary church worship and mission. The worksheet asks pupils to select what they would, and would not, include in a Gospel in the light of what they have learned about a Gospel's purpose.

Through this work pupils may further engage in work that considers the importance of religious experience and faith in interpreting and understanding such figures as Jesus. Hopefully pupils will begin to see the contexts in which the Gospels came into existence and a little of their contribution to the development of the faith.

Jesus as a personality

To see clearly some of the images the Gospels evoke of the personality of Jesus

Method

His reported effect on others around him provides interesting material for consideration.

Thus such stories as the callings of Simon Peter and of Levi are used. There is scope for drama activities and improvisation as well as more conservative written or discussion work.

Jesus the what? Considering the resurrection

To make pupils familiar with claims about Jesus made by Christians and others with particular reference to the resurrection stories

Method

Pupils should be able to recognise different claims made about Jesus, especially those made by Christians about Jesus 'the Christ'. Pupils should draw upon the preceding work in order to perform some type of evaluative tasks at an individual level. It is expected that staff will handle questions relating to faith issues sensitively. Pupils ought to be learning to treat such issues reasonably and sensibly.

Work for this section is based upon suggestions and reading in chapter 8 of the Chichester Project book, *Jesus*, by Trevor Shannon.

CONCLUSIONS TO THE THEME

This takes the form of a review of the work completed and the major conclusions each class feels able to make, if any!

I wish to explain one part of this course in some detail. This may make clearer what actually happens in the classroom.

JESUS IN ART

Nobody ever asked me to consider the role of, or purpose of, pictures of Jesus within the Christian community. Pictures of Jesus were used in schools and Sunday schools as a means to illuminate Gospel stories or to present fixed ideas about Jesus 'the Good Shepherd' who is 'meek and mild'. Even today there seems little doubt among school pupils that the historical Jesus bears a close resemblance to Robert Powell or Björn Borg!

Christian art has always had an important role to play within the life of the majority of Christians. This may relate to liturgical and devotional uses. It may also relate to the more subtle areas of personal experience and feelings. In this part of the course I wish to show that most pictures of Jesus attempt to convey 'truth' of a special kind, expressing what Jesus means to the believer. Such pictures are not, primarily, representational.

If Jesus is 'risen', is 'Lord', is the 'One who reveals God', then the function of Christian images of Christ will be to evoke something of this experience. If Jesus 'died for others', was a 'willing sacrifice', died 'abandoned by all but God', then the qualities of pathos and horror of art depicting the Passion will attempt to lead us through something of this experience. This is much as happens today on Palm Sunday. Many Christian congregations on that day read publicly and dramatically from the Passion story. In this way the faithful begin their own journey through Holy Week to the Cross and the experience of resurrection to a new life.

Early in the Jesus theme we consider 'pictures of Jesus'. Do they help us to know who or what Jesus is, or was? Are such pictures 'true'? If so, true in what sense?

All this is approached as follows:
(a) Using two selected slides of:
    (i) a Nazi anti-Jewish propaganda poster;
    (ii) The Duke of Wellington.
Pupils look in silence at each slide and then write a list containing ten words or phrases to describe in each case the 'man' in the picture.

Pupils tend to write down a mixture of what each one looks like and what each one's personality seems to be. From this, discussion arises about the pupils' perceptions and about the apparent aims of each artist. Portrait painters as much as poster designers are in the propaganda business. This may become clear to pupils.

I have also found it worth considering the differences between a painted portrait, a portrait photograph and a simple holiday snap of someone (or, similarly, a journalist's photograph of a person in the news). The TV programme *Spitting Image* can also provide ideas at this stage.

(b) Using three or four selected slides depicting Jesus, pupils are asked to give five words or phrases to describe the Jesus in each one. If the picture contains more than one person, it has proved interesting to invite pupils to talk about how they identify Jesus in the picture.

*Picture 12 De Eeurige Jood (The Eternal Jew), Nazi
film poster used in the occupied
Netherlands (source unknown)*

*Picture 13   The Duke of Wellington by Thomas
Lawrence (Picture by courtesy of the
Wellington Museum, Aspley House,
London)*

In this activity pupils are beginning to reflect upon the disparity of artistic presentations of Jesus. This is particularly true of pictures of non-European origin such as those shown on pp.3—4 of Trevor Shannon's book, *Jesus*.

At this stage pupils are encouraged to ask why the artists produced their pictures — what is each one trying to do? What is of the most importance in each one? How might each be used? If possible, an icon could be produced, especially if a picture of such an image being revered is available.

(c) In the third stage of this part of the work, pupils are expected to read pp.1—4 of Trevor Shannon's *Jesus*. In addition to selective use of the questions on p.5, the following are put to the pupils:

(i) Can we actually know what Jesus looked like? How can we know?

(ii) Does it matter if we can or cannot know what Jesus looked like? Give reasons for your answer.

(iii) Pick three of the pictures (in your textbook). Do any of these try to show what Jesus looked like? Explain your answer.

(iv) Draw, or cut out, from old magazines, or cards, one or more pictures of Jesus, and mount them in your exercise book. For each of your pictures say what sort of person the Jesus in it seems to be. For what reason or purpose do you think the picture was made?

Pupils do need to be told quite clearly that there is no contemporary description of Jesus' physical appearance, in written form or otherwise. Discussion and reading should have made this clear. Pupils are here introduced to pictures as a means of communicating faith and feelings and as a means of affecting others.

Experience has shown how successful this part of the whole scheme can be in stimulating critical thought within mixed-ability groups. It has not been unusual for genuine flashes of insight to occur amid lively argument, or because of irritation or surprise. None the less, in a mixed-ability setting it must be admitted that the effectiveness of any work is relative to a pupil's ability and motivation. Not surprisingly, we are constantly seeking more effective approaches with the less able in mind.

Resources: in this part of the course the main resources referred to have been:
Jesus by Trevor Shannon (Chichester Project Book 4, published by Lutterworth Press, Cambridge, 1982).
Christ in Art by Brenda Lealman (slide pack and notes with optional cassette, published by CEM, London, 1984.)

HOW THEN TO IMPROVE THE COURSE?

The frustrating thing about teaching Religious Studies is that one is never able to keep up with the range of new resources and ideas available. However, five areas of improvement are currently high on the list of priorities.

Resources

There is a need to introduce the new and good resources recently made available. The Mary Glasgow Publications resource pack, *Christianity* (filmstrips, cassettes, teachers' notes, and worksheets booklet) has made a major contribution to resources on Christianity. Filmstrip IIb of the pack ('Will the real Jesus please stand up') could be incorporated into the scheme immediately. Other publications, especially from CEM, are worthy of consideration (especially *Christ, Who's That?*, *The Image of Life* and *The Bible — A Story?*).

The Jesus of faith

Even more opportunity needs to be given to explore the 'faith-claims' of Christians about Jesus. What is his significance for them? How is he experienced? How does he affect their lives? Again, the Mary Glasgow *Christianity* pack and the CEM *Christ, Who's That?* booklet can help. Interviews with believers and others with opinions about Jesus may well follow. A greater use of art forms such as poetry and music could be seriously considered.

Group work

Even greater use could be made of structured small-group work as a means to further active pupil participation.

Jesus through non-Christian eyes

Some hesitant steps have been made to introduce some of the non-Christian ideas and attitudes about Jesus to be found around the world. Discovering a Jewish, Hindu, Buddhist or humanist viewpoint could bring a further dimension to the scheme.

Reading

Greater stimulus could be given to pupils to read more. In mixed-ability teaching it is too easy to overlook such matters. None the less, I recognise that encouragement to read more widely and independently is an important task of the teacher of Religious Education.

19 Classroom practice in RE

David Naylor

Religious educators have been well served by scholars who have clearly articulated the place of RE in the curriculum. *Religious Education in Hampshire Schools* (1978) and *Paths to Understanding* (1980) have given teachers a clear mandate for their professional role. The major task for the next decade is to narrow the gap between statements of ideals and actual practice in the classroom. Making religious insights accessible to pupils of a wide range of abilities, and in varying social contexts, is a mammoth undertaking.

This article considers, firstly, what needs to be provided by the school and, secondly, what methods may be employed by the teacher in order to promote interest and learning. Examples are taken mainly from Christianity, the teaching of which poses, in the experience of many teachers, particularly acute problems at the present time.

THE LEARNING CONTEXT

Many teachers work in difficult circumstances and it is no easy task to create a good learning environment. If, however, the learning experiences recommended in the units which follow are to be available it will be necessary to work towards a situation where adequate provision is made of the following:

Time

The minimum time required if RE is to have any real chance of success is 5 per cent of curriculum time (i.e. 2 periods a week in a 40 period week). In general, double periods would give more scope for the kind of pupil activity recommended in this volume. A fair test of the adequate provision of time is to count the weekly pupil turnover of each teacher; if this exceeds

400, the teacher is unlikely even to get to know the names of all the pupils for whom he or she is responsible.

Finance

Capitation allowance should be granted to RE on a *per capita* basis. A quick calculation will reveal the amount of money allocated to teach one pupil for a year. Its adequacy should be measured against an equivalent Humanities subject.

Accommodation

A room with facilities for the presentation of visual material is needed (without inconvenience), so that full use may be made of resources now available. A simple system of storage and retrieval, for book and non-book material, is essential to the survival of the busy teacher. Basic equipment should include a filing cabinet with space for translucent slide containers; plenty of open shelving; easy access to a projector on a stand; an overhead projector on a trolley; display space and a poster rack; a cassette recorder and tray units for general storage.

The seating plan in the classroom can either help or hinder the teaching style. A layout which enables pupils to communicate with each other as well as with the teacher has considerable advantages: for example the 'conference' style layout below has much to commend it because it enables work in pairs and small groups to occur without disruption, as well as being suitable for more formal didactic teaching.

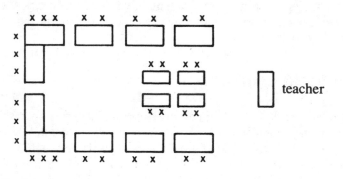

Picture 14 *Seating plan*

Correlation with other subjects

The achievement of the objectives of RE will be aided if teachers of the subject can enlist the co-operation of other subject areas, especially English, Home Economics, Drama, Art, Music, History and Geography. For example, work on a Christian festival involves becoming familiar with the basic story, looking at various customs and celebrations, thinking about the use of signs and symbols, and exploring inner meanings. If pupils prepare symbolic food in Home Economics, and in Art represent ideas using a variety of media, the work in RE is reinforced. Similarly, the development of the skills used in interpreting myth, symbol, allegory and poetry requires the co-operation of the English department. Religious expression takes many forms and logically its exploration requires a range of skills to which many colleagues can make a contribution.

LEARNING EXPERIENCE

Most RE departments, in documenting the course they offer, refer mainly to the content of the course preceded by a general statement of aims and objectives. It would be more useful to teachers if each stage were preceded by objectives specific to it, and if a third section on appropriate learning experiences were added. The school's RE syllabus would thus supply answers, relevant to each stage or age range, to three questions:

Why is this part of the course being taught? (i.e. the rationale)

What content is involved? (i.e. the programme)

How is this content to be made accessible to the pupils? (i.e. the learning experience)

The third of these questions has perhaps been given insufficient attention both in recent literature about the subject and in documents prepared by individual school departments. The remainder of this article offers some practical suggestions, many of which are expanded and exemplified in the other articles within this section.

Thinking skills

It is salutary for the teacher to reflect on his own attendance at lectures and to consider the length of his own attention span, and a few days later to articulate clearly the extent of his learning. This may help self-evaluation in considering the effectiveness of exposition as a learning device in the classroom. Learning processes which engage all the pupils in the class need to be devised. Techniques recommended by Edward de Bono in *Teaching Thinking* (Hounslow, Temple Smith, 1976) can be useful devices for the RE teacher. Working in pairs or small groups to brainstorm a topic; writing down the good, bad and interesting points about a statement or picture; ranking a set of statements in order of their importance: such activities can engage pupils more fully than trying to hold a discussion with a whole class. For example, pupils might be asked to write all they know about 'The Bible' or 'Jesus': the result will enable the teacher to see areas of need and to match subsequent lessons to these needs. Work on texts can make good use of thinking skills: e.g. pupils might list what they consider to be the good, bad and interesting points about the injunction 'Love your enemies'. The exercise challenges them to think, and discussion of their own ideas should lead to a deeper understanding of the attitude and teaching of Jesus.

Learning through visual stimuli

Most filmstrips and slide sets are too long. The temptation to 'get through them' is strong, but should be resisted as likely to be unproductive. Presentation of carefully selected slides, accompanied by questions which will engage the pupil with the thoughts, feelings, symbols and actions portrayed, can take the pupil to the central ideas more effectively than if he is a passive viewer. The same applies to video tapes, for where classes simply watch, the level of understanding is lower than when the teacher (judiciously using a remote control) focuses attention on central issues and sets appropriate tasks. Pupils can be asked to observe closely certain significant features, which may then be discussed. In a visual presentation of the Christian Eucharist, for example, attention may be directed towards the role played by one particular individual. Speculation, in pairs, about his feelings and intentions can enable pupils to penetrate beyond the outward features of the rite into the meanings enshrined in it. Reference to the use of symbolic representation and action in another faith can sharpen awareness still further.

Learning from visitors

A visitor should be regarded as a valuable resource rather than as a substitute teacher. The ideal is to plan for a series of visitors, representing between them a range of commitments. Emotionally-charged offerings need not be avoided, for they are an important part of the kaleidoscope of religious expression; but unprepared encounters with people who have some idiosyncratic message to put across are difficult to justify educationally. Visitors should always be clearly briefed, and be aware that pupils will be encouraged to enter into reasoned dialogue with them. Preparation for a visitor is essential, and might well include the gathering of background information and the formulation, after discussion, of key questions to be put to the visitor by the pupils and the teacher. The teacher — not the visitor — should be fully in charge of the proceedings.

Learning from visits

Visits to places of worship are recommended, in principle, but visits to empty, cold churches may be counter-productive (as may tours guided by the minister). Religious buildings, however much they may appeal as historic monuments containing beautiful artefacts and symbols of the faith, are essentially convenient meeting places used by communities of people trying to live out their faith. It is essential therefore for pupils to encounter people and to question them about what the place of worship and its community mean to them. It hardly needs saying that, as far as the building and it symbols are concerned, finding out is better than being told, and questions are better answered after they have been asked rather than before. If arrangements can be made for pupils, during their visit, to experience some of the activities typical of the worship of the community, the visit will be more fruitful. (For further suggestions see (1980) *Paths to Understanding*, Basingstoke, Macmillan, pp.27ff.)

Learning from simulation and artefacts

The RE teacher is neither priest nor guru, but educator. When launching any simulated activity (e.g. baptism, meditation, marriage, etc.) he needs to make his intention clear to his pupils. Throughout he needs to act as a commentator and to encourage discussion. Religious leaders who are 'at home' with young people may be available to help. Religious artefacts can be used effectively to arouse curiosity. The idea that symbols are 'silent teachers' points pupils to the history and the meanings enshrined in the artefacts, as well as to the devotion which they elicit from the believer. Always in this kind of work emphasis should be placed on the meaning which ritual and symbol hold for the adherent, rather than on mere information. For example, reflection about memories and associations could be followed by pupils speculating about the meaning likely to be enshrined in, for example, a rosary, an icon or the burning of incense. If the artefacts can then be discussed with someone for whom they are important, the lesson is likely to develop the pupils' capacity for empathy.

Reading texts and story-telling

Where the dramatic impact of a story or text is vital, it is rarely successful to hand over the task of reading to the class volunteer. Using different versions, telling the story in your own words, and playing tapes of famous actors reading all have their place. There is a case for 'story time' at the end of a lesson without any reflection or discussion. Usually, however, discussion about interpretations reinforces the essential point that stories have many levels of meaning. The exegesis of texts, a familiar element in courses of study in higher education, may sometimes be appropriate provided that it does not inhibit the more imaginative and divergent ideas which come from some pupils. Teachers with strong yet relaxed discipline and adequate facilities can attempt drama as a way of deepening pupils' insight into stories. Exploration of the inner meaning of stories or parables in mime, movement or drama is more likely to be effective than a mere telling of the story. For example, exploring themes such as reconciliation or jealousy may be more effective than acting out the story of the Prodigal Son.

Worksheets

There has been a tendency in recent years to over-use these, for even an imaginatively-conceived booklet, produced with the greatest do-it-yourself skill, is hard put to catch the pupils' interest and compete with the many cleverly designed materials now commercially available. Where worksheets are used they should direct the pupils to a wider range of learning experiences linked with other resources. It is also useful to check that the cognitive level of operation demanded of the pupil goes beyond mere comprehension, that it stimulates the imagination, and that it demands such skills as analysis and evaluation. (Bloom's *Taxonomy of Educational Objectives, Vol. 1 Cognitive Domain* is still a valuable guide.) For example, a worksheet on worship could involve looking at a slide in a hand-viewer, identifying the key symbols, and ranking a set of statements about meanings according to their importance.

Careful reflection on each of the above issues should help to make Religious Education, in general, and the teaching of Christianity, in particular, more effective.

20 Teaching Christianity: Assessment and Examinations

Alan Brown

ASSESSMENT

Assessment is a broad concept which affects examinations but goes much deeper into the aim of education itself. It is as well to begin with the key to all assessment – aims and objectives. If the pupil is to be assessed then there have to be clear criteria by which the pupil's progress should be measured.

Christianity is not a collection of information, hence one cannot test a pupil's understanding of Christianity through knowledge alone. Knowledge can be tested by memory, verbal fluency etc., but understanding must lie deeper. How can one assess a pupil's understanding of Chrisianity in a religious sense? I would suggest that this cannot be easily achieved, just as it is not easy to measure anyone's commitment to any religion. Perhaps one way towards a deeper understanding is to engage the pupil in some experimental activity that will help her/him become more aware of what it means to be a Christian. This does not mean a 'confessional' approach to Christianity – nothing could be more closed – rather it means that the pupil will recognise that to be religious (or in this case Christian) means more than collecting information and being able to regurgitate it.

One may illustrate this through Clive Erricker's use of pictures juxtaposed with biblical text in *Christian Experience* (Cambridge, Lutterworth Press, 1982). Here Erricker uses the feelings and emotions expressed within each picture to open up a familiar text. There is no 'correct' answer, for the pupils are invited to respond personally to the text by relating two art forms. It is a recognition that the understanding of a biblical text will be complemented by one's own experience and the experience of others; it is not a purely cognitive activity. John Rankin in *The Eucharist* (Cambridge, Lutterworth Press, 1985) adopts a simple technique of pupils breaking bread with each other and talking. A simple act, but one in which he tries to help the pupil recognise the fellowship that is a key feature of the Christian celebration of the Eucharist. Here Rankin is not concerned to re-enact the Eucharist but simply to capture something of the feelings shared by the Christians who participate in the ritual.

These types of activity in the classroom involve an element of risk for the teacher. It is extremely difficult to assess a pupil's understanding of Christianity when approached through feelings and emotions. The teacher can become unsure as to how the objectives of each lesson can be assessed because the means of testing is simply not directly available. The whole assessment process appears to rest upon literary ability, and how fluently or accurately a pupil responds to a particular question. If one is to allow the pupil the freedom and flexibility to explore the affective nature of Christianity, then the teacher will need some confidence in her/his teaching strategy. The history of Christianity is littered with devout believers who have expressed their faith through painting, sculpture or music, on the basis of her/his expertise in the creative arts. The educational world seems to be happier assessing a pupil's ability with words rather than her/his ability to express herself in other creative ways.

The teacher also has to have the courage to re-define what is often called 'knowledge'. One can assess whether pupils have learned a series of facts but part of the knowledge they acquire is the method by which the subject (or knowledge) is transmitted. Teachers, like all of us, feel secure in being able to justify a mark, be it out of ten or a hundred, but often real learning cannot be quantified, nor should it be. The security lies in the system which recognises success through achievement in written examinations, and this has a direct effect on the teaching methods and strategies used in years 7-9 of the secondary school.

Pupil Assessment

There are at least two broad areas of assessment. One is the assessment of each pupils' knowledge and evaluative skills; the way in which pupils handle material and are able to demonstrate the ability to think and reflect.

These skills are in many ways no different from that developed in other subjects. There are of course skills that are distinctive to Religious Education (although this is by no means uniformly agreed) and one would expect some of those listed below to be among those to be assessed during the pupils time in school.

(a) the perception and recognition of religious beliefs and values in the secular world together with an evaluation and articulation of these;

(b) the ability to recognise religious concepts and identify the application of them in *practice.*

(c) the ability to illustrate concepts and apply them in certain situations;

(d) the recognition that evaluation and analysis of religious phenomena may have a direct and pressing relevance to the social, political, environmental order;

(e) relating behaviour to beliefs and values;

(f) the exploration of platitudes often connected with religious/moral issues and the exposing of these;

and more generally:

(g) the acquisitions of skills valuable to many aspects of adult life;

(h) the exploration of some issues in particular depth;

(i) Religious Studies contribution to 'deepening and broadening' of the skills, ability, knowledge and aptitude of the students.

Teacher's Self-Assessment

The other broad area of assessment should be the teacher's own self assessment. There is little point in assessing the pupil's ability if the teacher has not provided the pupil with the means to be assessed. Teachers do need to reflect on their own professional competence and ensure that they provide not just information but situations which encourage reflection, imagination and creativity.

They could, amongst many other things, be expected to provide opportunities for the pupil to:

(a) express his or her knowledge in a variety of ways;

(b) reflect upon specific experiences;

(c) demonstrate an ability to evaluate information;

(d) recognise that 'atmosphere' is a powerful ingredient in religious practice;

(e) be still and silent;

(f) identify and appreciate the creative skills of people who had responded to the religious way of life;

(g) recognise the diversity of religious expression.

A significant number of pupils do not respond to the normally accepted means of assessment. Something may be in the pupil's mind seeking a mode of expression, but the pupil does not have the facility to express herself/himself. It is with this in view that it seems appropriate for one model of assessment, one level of targets for attainment if you like, to relate to the teacher. I would like to suggest that as well as drawing up programmes of study, targets for attainment etc. that each *teacher* in each class draws up a 'Strategy for Teaching'.

This should be based upon affirmative answers to the following questions:

(i) Have I ensured that all pupils know what is expected of them?

(ii) Have I provided a range of assessment models for the pupils during the course of the year?

(iii) Have I created an environment in the classroom which has been conducive to learning?

(iv) Have I encouraged a range of skills to be developed in the pupils i.e. literary, artistic, listening?

(v) Have I represented the religious tradition(s) I have taught in a way they would find acceptable?

(vi) Have I helped pupils to experience something of the range of feelings and emotions that are expressed in the religion(s) studied through music, art, sculpture, drama and the visual and creative arts?

No doubt one could continue saying what other people should do but there is little point in drawing up complex and detailed matrices relating to pupil achievement and assessment unless teachers are more self-critical about their own strategies for teaching and pupil's learning. A pupil may be bursting to express a view on some issue but has only been 'allowed' to write an essay, fill in a missing word, or voice an opinion. Surely they should be encouraged to 'collect', 'classify', 'create', 'listen', etc. Not in every lesson, nor every week perhaps, but if these diverse teaching methods are absent throughout a whole programme of study, it is the teacher who is failing – not the pupil. However, it will be the pupil who will be seen to fail. This is one of the unacceptable features of teaching which is often comfortably ignored.

In other words assessment is not simply about Key Stages 1-4, it includes the pupil's personal development and the nurturing of a sense of religious (or spiritual) awareness. The teacher and the RE scheme of work needs not just to allow, but positively to encourage pupils to explore the varieties of religious experience.

There have been a number of attempts to resolve the issue of assessment in RE. None of them are wholly convincing because they all wrestle with clarifying the aims and assessment objectives of RE. If RE is largely concerned with content, it is then a relatively simple matter to assess a pupil's ability to remember and/or understand that content. However, RE burdens itself with a belief that it has to affect pupils and as soon as that affective area enters the assessment arena, normal criteria of assessment fly out of the window. As long as RE wants the best of both worlds – informational and affective – then it will never resolve the problems of assessment.

EXAMINATIONS

What should examinations assess? Perhaps a more pertinent question is 'How should examinations assess?' Recent changes in the GCSE RS criteria have introduced new syllabuses and we will have to wait to see if the lessons of the last few years have been learned. Certainly some syllabuses still seem to sprawl across the page, not giving teachers or pupils clarity about what is expected.

In-spite of criticism from some quarters who imply the contrary, the vast majority of pupils at GCSE sit a paper on Christianity. One of the most popular papers is that on 'Christian Ethics' or some similarly titled syllabus. The problem for assessment here is essentially two fold. One really is clarity:

'Do you think that the termination of life is ever justified? Give reasons for your answer'.

Here there is ambiguity of language. Is the question about euthanasia, abortion, capital punishment, killing in war etc.? Unless the candidate is fortunate enough to have access to the marking scheme she (or he) is placed in an impossible situation. That gloomy situation is intensified because the sophistication necessary for a sixteen year old to deal with this very complex question is rarely found among that age range.

The question is unfair (a) because it is not clear and (b) because it is too large a question to be dealt with adequately in the limited time available. In passing one might note that this type of question is much more prevalent in Christianity papers than in papers on the other world religions.

Another example is instanced by the cartoon below:

Look at the cartoon below and answer the question which follows.

'... and on earth peace, goodwill toward men'

(a) Why has the artist drawn the sign with one letter missing?

The idea of positive stimulus is still relatively new and examination boards are still experimenting, but this picture indicates that the examiners may not understand 15-16 year old humour nor may they be aware that the picture could be unhelpful to the lower ability candidate.

Actually the question is very demanding and raises a number of serious issues about Christmas but no one *really* knows what was in the artist's mind.

(i) 'Do you think the events of a person's life are pre-ordained by God?
(ii) 'Name two feast days which commemorate events in the life of Jesus'

Would it have been better if, in (i), 'already decided' have been used in place of 'pre-ordained' and, in (ii) 'commemorate' changed to 'remember'?

So clarity of language, comprehensible, stimulating, jargon-free, plain English together with a concise focus would improve the quality of examinations for the pupil. The best example of an unfocused question comes not from Christianity but from a Judaism paper.

'State five facts about the Torah'.

The marking scheme allowed trivial information to receive as much credit as significant facts. It would have been much better to have qualified the type of facts required and built a proper differentiation into the marking of the question. An example of this is:

'The Sabbath is described as a holy day'
Is this an accurate description? Give reasons (5)

Marking Schemes
Focus: Evaluation of Sabbath as a holy day?
One reason give (1)
At least two reasons given (2-3)
At least three reasons given in developed form (4-5)
Examples of reasons
- Set apart for God
- Different activities compared to rest of week
- Time of worship
- no work

Assessment and examinations are linked. They both have a long way to go before they can do justice to Christianity as a world religion. Perhaps they raise problems which can never be properly resolved because of the endemic relationship between Christianity and English culture. Most RE books still come from a Christian environment, if not from a particular denomination, and use Christian assumptions that remain extremely difficult to identify and eradicate. Examination boards will respond to changes in RE but they also have the responsibility to re-define their questions to ensure that the teaching of Christianity is not examined on the basis of normative assumptions associated with the faith, but through the variety of educational methods used in other subjects. New agreed syllabuses have tried to develop a variety of modes of assessment and self assessment e.g. FARE, DARE but the difficulty of defining assessment in 'non-religion-specific' terms remains extremely complex and one has to await further developments.

21 Teaching Christianity: process and purpose

Mary Hayward

Christianity should be the easiest area in the RE curriculum to provide resources for! There can be few schools whose immediate environment offers no possibility of a visit to a church or chapel; no possibility of an encounter with individual Christians or a Christian community; and bears no mark of Christian influence or activity. But of course timetabling and school organisation militate against firsthand experience as the medium of learning an anything more than an infrequent basis. Moreover, children's experience outside school may well lie within other religious traditions, or outside all, So Christianity — and indeed other faiths — encountered in the classroom are inevitably several stages removed from reality. Resources which can communicate effectively become vital: they must *adequately express* what is involved in 'being a Christian', and they must *adequately engage* the pupil in his or her attempt to understand this.

At this point readers may like to pause and make two lists: the first list should note the resources you would ideally like to have to hand for teaching about Christianity; the second, the resources regularly in use at your school. Work in an RE centre would suggest that video might 'top' the first list, whilst books — with slides or filmstrips as supplementary material from time to time — would 'top' the second. The latter would be accompanied by some qualifying statement expressing the conviction that many books are inadequate, usually because they fail to engage the children for whom they are intended. In the field of RE, books still dominate the resources available for schools, and publishers clearly see a promising market in RE. Books, therefore, provide the main focus for discussion here; they are also the focus because they frequently constitute a packaging of material which I believe is 'tighter' than that of other media. As well as offering specific content, they offer *directives for learning activities: they expressly indicate a process*. Of course, it is also the case that the learning process(es) advocated by any textbook is not confined to 'pupil activities'.

Books are expensive! It is useful therefore to consider criteria which might be used in their selection. A headline in a *TES Extra* on Geography caught my eye. It said simply 'Selecting the Best', and its author noted that 'the "textbooks are dead" prophets have died, not the textbooks.' I read on:

> The good textbook has a great *variety* of *interesting* and *practicable* pupils' activities from which to choose. The bad textbook merely provides the information and provides for regurgitation. (My *italics*) (Wright, D. (14 December 1984)) 'Selecting the Best', in *The Times Educational Supplement*)

I warmed to this! And to this:

> Some textbooks look so unattractive that they seem to come from the era when only unpleasant things were thought to be good for you. (Op. cit.)

And comfortably confirming a suspicion I had for a long time (not that I expect to find universal agreement — but it's good for teachers to know their own likes and dislikes!):

> On the other hand textbooks which look like comics do not appeal to teachers or pupils, many pupils find them patronizing, silly, and a waste of time. (Op. cit.)

RE books in both categories come readily to mind! But the main thrust of this *TES* article was to suggest criteria for choosing a textbook. All the criteria were very pragmatic: some clearly related to 'hard times' — cost, durability, design and printing; others to children's engagement — the variety of resources found within a textbook, colour (distinct from design and printing), the conceptual level and language level, the values and bias (presumably hidden and overt) and the suggested range of pupil activities.

It is with the issue of engagement that we are concerned here, and thus with the *learning processes which may both enable the teacher to fulfil the purposes (aims) he or she has and give purpose to the children as they study*. In speaking of a process of learning — or processes — in books, it is useful to look beyond the activities set, as well as at them! There are thus four areas which I suggest are worth exploring and which are taken up in this chapter: the book's resources, the conceptual and language levels, the values and bias, and pupil activities.

SEARCH FOR RESOURCES WITHIN THE RESOURCE!

> The *TES* article suggested pupils might be involved in the assessment of books: It is a good exercise for pupils to examine textbooks for the variety of resources, and it need not take long. Working in pairs, pupils list every type of resource they can find in a textbook. The resultant list provides a good definition of the scope of modern geography. (We might substitute RE.) (Op. cit.)

I tested this notion on two of the Chichester Project books.[1] The two lists in the table — neither exhaustive — indicate the range of resources with which a student is required to work.

CHRISTIAN WORSHIP	CHRISTIAN ETHICS
Photographs: very varied of worship	Story
Artefacts: e.g. rosary; crib; breviary	Extracts from literature
	Photographs
Sculpture	'Parable'
Paintings	Problem situations
Buildings	Posters
Creed	Personal statements
Prayers	Art
Prayer books	Poetry
Scriptural passages	Maps
Hymns	Case study (El Salvador)
'Offices'	Newspaper extracts
Calendar	Letters
Music	Eyewitness accounts
Visits	'Rich Poor Game'

Of course, the content of both lists is presented in words, illustrations and pictures in the books, but it indicates for the teacher a wide range of resources which may be used in undertaking a study in either area. From the pupils' perspective it is clear that this wide range of resources holds greater potential for involvement and engagement. Pupil and teacher are also directed beyond the confines of the book — a visit can be made; music can be listened to; photographs can be taken; a rosary can be carefully handled; and newspaper cuttings collected. And, importantly, in encountering each resource, different demands are made on students. Moreover, the range of resources not only 'rings true' in the sense that it begins to reflect the riches of Christian worship — or the complexities of decision-making in personal and social ethics — but a wide range of material is more likely to offer interest to more children. As a simple example, I observed a second year mixed-ability group involved in a study of Jesus and the Gospels while they were engaged in a variety of tasks. Encountering some parallel passages in the synoptic gospels proved a source of interest to a group of 'bright' boys who wanted to pursue the matter; on the other hand, a lesson which looked at images of Jesus in art and invited verbal and written responses provoked greater interest and perceptive comments from quite a different group of children who were not among the most able in the class.

A CASE STUDY: VISUAL RESOURCES

Watching out for the range of resources a book offers may be useful. It is also worth asking how the resources you identify function in the book, and more importantly, in the learning process (the two are not necessarily the same!). Pictures appear in most textbooks and we have already noted that they may direct us to the other resources (a building, an artefact or a book of prayers, for example), so here we will focus on pictures in their own right. What must be considered? I would suggest that, firstly, there is a cluster of questions about *presentation* which are very basic. Are the pictures big enough to be useful? Is it better to have fewer pictures, but excellent quality? Are they of a quality which will attract interest and comment (of the positive kind!)? Certainly, answers here will relate to the usefulness of pictures in the learning process.

Does it matter if books don't have colour? Do children expect colour, and does it affect interest and attitude? Is colour so much a part of religion that I do a disservice to the richness of the Orthodox tradition if I show a picture of an iconostasis in black and white? Or consider the colour of the stone of a cathedral, even that may have a story to tell: of where it was brought from and why, at what personal cost and care, and with what motivation and purpose? At present I can think of only three recent series of textbooks (as opposed to 'information' books) which offer colour.[2] A further question here is that of artists' impressions versus photographs. It is important to decide where your own preference lies. I know I would prefer to *use* photographs of the ruins of the synagogue in Capernaum, rather than an artist's reconstruction, but I'd be prepared to 'make do' with the latter. But do I want artists' impressions relating to the Beatitudes? I think not. Or of the Psalms?[3] No! (Although I might encourage pupils to explore both examples visually themselves, e.g. through collage.) Can an artist's impression sometimes pre-empt thought and imagination — and thus engagement? If so, another practical task is to note how a book makes use of them.

Secondly, we may ask how visuals function in a text: what they actually *do* should be *intentional*, that is, they are there to fulfil a purpose which bears on the learning process. Intentional use of pictures in RE textbooks may include the following points.

(a) Pictures may be used to *illustrate a specific aspect of the text*. This is probably the most common use.

(b) Pictures may *function* as a text. For example, *People* in the *Exploring Religion* series (London, Bell & Hyman, 1984) considers the work of an Anglican priest, Bill Ind. The written text is largely Bill Ind 'speaking'. The pictures (in the space of twelve pages) tell of the following aspects of his work: with youth, with the youth group, with the choir, with families, with the sick, his preaching, his reading of the Bible, his personal prayer, his celebration of the Eucharist, his work in Sunday school and day school, and his preparation of a young couple for marriage.

(c) Pictures may *extend a text*. Thus, for example, the pictures of Iona in Alan Brown's *Christian Communities* (Cambridge, Lutterworth Press, 1982) give a sense of place, whilst those on Easter in *The Christian World* (London, Macdonald, 1984) by the same author, extend the reader's horizons beyond the celebration of the festival in western churches.

(d) Pictures may *offer insights which words alone cannot so adequately convey*. They may be more powerful than words. This is probably true of the use of 'works of art'. One recent RE textbook uses Gauguin's *D'où venons-nous? Que sommes-nous? Où allons-nous?* as its starting point;[4] Clive Erricker draws on the work of Grant Wood, Henri Rousseau, Salvador Dali, Pablo Picasso, Graham Sutherland, Georges Rouault, William Blake and Stanley Spencer in his two books for the Chichester Project. He writes of *using* pictures elsewhere in this book. But good photographic material may function in this way too. Reflect, for example, on pictures which perhaps stand out in your mind from Christian Aid or Oxfam, or the Salvation Army or any number of charitable organisations. Do they have a power beyond words? Do they offer new insights?[5]

(e) Pictures may be *expressly used in a text to engage pupils in specific tasks.* Here pictures are explicitly used as a part of the learning process. In *Christian Ethics* (Cambridge, Lutterworth Press, 1984), Clive Erricker asks students to study three pictures:

> The first is a photograph of Che Guevara the communist guerilla leader shortly after his death in Bolivia. The second is Egyptian. It is of Anubis, protector of the dead person, supervising his journey to the afterlife. The third is an impression of resurrection.* What do each of these three pictures suggest to you about death? Give a caption to each one starting
> "Death is ..." (Erricker, C. (1984) *Christian Ethics*, Cambridge, Lutterworth Press)
> (**The Resurrection, Cookham* by Stanley Spencer)

Such intentional uses of pictures in RE textbooks clearly relate to the learning process, not just to their function in the book as such. The criteria offered here are not exhaustive. They offer a starting-point for assessing the part visuals play in published materials. Oddly, RE textbooks scrutinised on the basis of criteria (d) and (e) do not score very highly. Even a book about Christianity presented in words *and pictures* includes very little use of pictures when examined from the perspective of (e).[6] Of course, the absence of this explicit purpose in a textbook does not mean that a teacher may not use the pictures in this way with his or her class, but I would suggest that the book which has faced this issue from the outset is more likely to have the kind of pictures which will in fact be *useful.*

CONSIDERING THE WRITTEN TEXT

> Most textbooks use unnecessarily complex vocabulary and sentence structure. Preference should be given to books which pupils can read and understand without difficulty. (Wright, D. op. cit.)

Of course this is of immediate concern to the teacher in assessing books for his or her pupils. If the English is too complex, and if the style is dull, if it talks down to children, if it pretends to use their codes, or if the print is small and densely-packed on the page − learning will be affected. We have already spoken about the *presentation* of visuals, so, in a similar way, we can speak of how words are 'packaged' and this includes the quality of the English, style, and the visual presentation of the words.

Concrete concepts?

> Simplicity of language must not however be confused with simplicity of content:
> Provided the examples are concrete, the conceptual level can probably be higher than

CONCRETE EXPERIENCES

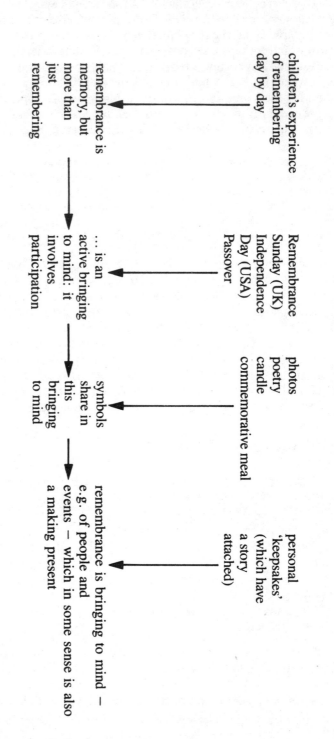

children's experience of remembering day by day

Remembrance Sunday (UK) Independence Day (USA) Passover

photos poetry candle commemorative meal

personal 'keepsakes' (which have a story attached)

remembrance is memory, but more than just remembering

... is an active bringing to mind: it involves participation

symbols share in this bringing to mind

remembrance is bringing to mind — e.g. of people and events — which in some sense is also a making present

CONCEPTUAL UNDERSTANDING

Picture 15 Building a concept: remembrance

in the past: today's 11 year olds who may have watched *John Craven's Newsround* with interest and growing comprehension for three years or more do not appreciate the assumption that they know little and understand even less about the world. (Wright, D. op. cit.)

Children can be grossly underestimated. Most teachers will be able to think of at least one child who seemed quite incapable of coping with 'their' subject, but whose knowledge and understanding in some other area — perhaps an individual interest or hobby — far outshone what was ever asked or expected of him or her in school. The marvellous passage in *Kes* where Billy speaks to his spellbound peers — and teacher — of his handling of Kes illustrates the same point.[7] There are many messages for the teacher here — but we are concerned to stress that clear expression does not necessarily preclude stretching the pupil, and *providing examples are concrete the conceptual level can probably be higher than in the past.* Isn't this the case with the resurrection narratives? On the one hand, there is the concrete language of the resurrection stories, on the other, the concept of resurrection. For some the concrete story is *itself* all important; for others it is the story's affirmation of the resurrection which is decisive. This kind of distinction may be important for children at secondary level to begin to grasp. But the exploration of why Christians find the stories important, and of why they were a part of the earliest tradition, is arguably more important than the concrete story, even if it takes the teacher and the child into difficult conceptual territory. But books can sabotage such an enterprise:

> Resurrection means 'rising up'. Jesus rose from the dead to new life: *new because* (my *italics*) he could come and go suddenly through locked doors. (Thorley, S. (1984) *Christianity in Words and Pictures,* Exeter, RMEP)

Surely this is to be avoided (and other passages in the book suggest the author can't *really* have meant this). Such reinforcement of the concrete (excuse the expression!) actually hinders understanding. What is new is surely *not* coming and going through locked doors, but the first Christians' experience of Jesus' resurrection — and all that it implied — and their profound perception of Jesus' continuing presence with them, a presence not limited by time and space.

It is also worth considering how books may help children to *build concepts.* *Remembrance* is important in any discussion of the Eucharist, and although it would be possible for a tidy dictionary definition of remembrance to be given (and some books operate in this way) a text which explores remembrance will have more to offer. John Rankin's *The Eucharist* (Lutterworth Press, 1985) does just this. The flow diagram (Picture 15) indicates the development of the concept in the book's text, a development reinforced by the activities suggested for pupils.

And of course in the classroom 'remembrance' might become a richer concept than this, as teacher and student interact and share experiences. A good text gives a lead, it is stimulating for teacher and student — and importantly it can help such 'concept-building'. Jill Paton Walsh, well known for her books for children, was recently interviewed on radio. She spoke of her personal enjoyment of talking with children, and, when questioned about the success of her books, commented that in writing she likes to hold in mind the possibilities, not the present limitations, of the children for whom she writes: perhaps writers of textbooks should take note!

The written text and patterns of teaching and learning

Many books for the RE market are 'information' or 'source' books, and while some of the criteria suggested above may certainly be used in the assessment of this kind of book, they are not the books I am primarily concerned with at this point. I want to look rather at those books which suggest a specific course of study. I selected five books and began to realise that written texts operate in different ways. Identifying these ways – in broad terms – may in turn be related to patterns of teaching and learning.

1. *Christian Ethics* (Cambridge, Lutterworth Press, 1984) In this book there is what I will term a *link text*: that is, it brings together a wide range of verbal and visual stimulus material into a coherent whole – it 'introduces', it sharpens issues, it poses questions, and it summarises.

2. *Christian Worship* (Cambridge, Lutterworth Press, 1982) Here the text serves the purpose of *providing information*, but with the learner firmly in mind. Concepts are built and there is an interplay between the pupil's experience and the phenomenon of worship. There is however a clear distinction between pupil activities and the text. The text is self-sufficient here, in a way in which the *link text* is not.

3. *Christian Communities* (Cambridge, Lutterworth Press, 1982) is not dissimilar to (2), but the text tells a story. Perhaps we can label this the *documentary text*. (This reader found it had resonances of TV documentaries!) Unquestionably it tells a 'real' story, for it is written in the present tense, and is often personal in tone – the writer is engaged with the subject matter himself!

4. *Christianity Then and Now* (Oxford, Oxford University Press, 1983) An opening note to the teacher refers to the double page spreads, which make up this book, as 'stories'. *The stories are large enough to stimulate the most able pupils while being simple enough to interest the less able.*[8] This story style is used indifferently to present material from a variety of sources: biblical, particular moments in history, cameos of the present, and biography. Story has its own inner power, but this is story as technique rather than as a creative force. Perhaps I may term this a *give-an-account-of text*. This description is I think reinforced by the 'Understanding your work' questions at the end of each spread.

5. *Christianity in words and pictures* (Exeter, RMEP, 1984) This book represents yet another way of how a text functions. Here, the text – which is quite slight if one looks just at the main blocks of writing – *provides information and explanation/interpretation*. It differs from *Christian Worship* in that the text *per se* does not invite the pupil to become involved, but is merely *instructive*.

It would perhaps be too simplistic to try and identify particular teaching styles and learning processes which correspond to these examples of how the text of a book may 'work', yet I do not think the idea is wholly fanciful. Like the present writer, readers may be able to recognise themselves as teachers in one or more of the above categories! And this is not insignificant for the choice of books the RE teacher makes, or for the variety of learning experiences that are offered to the children. And which kind of text is most likely to engage pupils in learning? Probably they should encounter a variety of texts – but if only one is available, which one? Does *education* demand more than personal preference?

ACTIVITIES

The earlier sections of this chapter have tried to illustrate that the process of learning is related to a book's whole structure, not just those sections variously labelled – 'Questions', 'Understand your work', 'Some thing(s) to do', 'Ask yourself', 'Further activities', 'Check your reading', 'Think spot', 'Use your imagination', 'Find out for yourself', 'Tasks', and 'Find out more' – which punctuate the textbooks (and surely deserve to be parodied!). However...

Activities and the teacher

Most teachers are glad at one time or another for a list of activities. At the same time most will have been infuriated by the impracticality of some of the suggested tasks – and their irrelevance to the students, the text, and the subject matter. To recognise this is probably to suggest that teachers are the best initiators of activities – not least because they know the children. This is particularly the case where tasks are less than integral to a book (arguably the case in examples 4 and 5, see p.163). And where tasks are integral, as is especially the case in example 1, and in the same author's *Christian Experience* (Cambridge, Lutterworth Press, 1982), the teacher may want to ask how his role as teacher is affected. Is it possible for a text to make the teacher redundant, for example? This would be an extreme example which is not apparent in the texts cited here – but even a shift in the direction of the teacher becoming a co-learner can cause discomfort! I suspect that this placing of 'activities' in a text may also provide the teacher with a clue to their importance within the book, and more importantly within the child's learning.

Activities and the child

If we turn to the child it is not simply a question of providing variety, interest and practicality, for tasks which meet these criteria, highlighted earlier, are important, but others come into play too. With the development of GCSE on a foundation of national criteria it is going to be important to ask at what level pupils are engaged when activities are set (and subsequently assessed). Knowledge, understanding and evaluation have emerged as three key words. Such criteria need to be operative – at appropriate levels – long before pupils embark on GCSE courses, and *can* be so!

So, imagine three questions about a rosary.

Questions	Possible Answers
What is a rosary? (knowledge)	A set of beads arranged in a special way and used by some Christians in prayer. (A fuller answer might give details of the arrangement and size of beads and mention the crucifix).
What does a rosary symbolise for a Christian and how is it used? (understanding)	A description would follow of use, of prayers spoken, and of the joys, mysteries and sorrows the beads recall for the Christian.
Why do you think that some Christians find the rosary helpful? (evaluation)	Answers might relate to concentration, focus, meditation on central Christian truths, discipline, the helpfulness of a set form of prayer.

But, when questions are a part of these activities, they often operate only at the level of knowledge — which may be synonymous with recall of the text. The example given here is in a sense too easy, as questions are the easiest activity to provide and criteria can and must underlie other tasks too.

Consider a group of children who, at the end of a course on church buildings and worship in the Christian community, are given the task of designing a church for their locality. Their brief tells them to consider carefully the people who will come to it, its use, its shape, and its furnishings and decoration. They must be prepared to present their plans to the class, and answer questions. A more imaginative task! But one requiring considerable knowledge and understanding, as well as evaluation skills (yet not necessarily dependent on writing skills). It is also a task which raises the issue of time allocation — and this is a further question a teacher may ask of the suggested activities in books. The foregoing reference to writing skills suggests also that activities should not always be equated with written work, as variety *is* important, certainly for the child — and for the teacher too who quickly wearies over thirty sets of identikit answers! Variety in activities is related to the range of resources in a book as we noted earlier. It is related too to the variety of children, which it appears hard for books to anticipate!

A further point is that children must be able to see that a task is worthwhile. 'Correct this statement', a feature of activities in *Christianity Then and Now*, may provide passing amusement by their absurdity:

T.S. Eliot runs a hamburger bar in Soho and is a famous writer of thrillers. (p.54)
The Sheriff of Nineveh welcomed Jonah with whisky and dancing girls. (p.54)

or give offence:

Toc H is a branch of the IRA which arranges for people to be shot. (p.66)
or startle readers by their total irrelevance − thus this reference to a fictitious
passage:

Dorothy Baker's brother, Sam, was minister of a Pentecostal church. (p.78)

I know, of course, that the technique is intended to reinforce and check
what children have learnt from the text. But the activity soon palls − though
the bright and the lazy would learn a lot about the use of negatives − and
such examples might even be considered downright misleading, or at best
confusing.

Christians wrote the New Testament to replace the Old Testament. (p.38)

The High Priest lived in the Holy of Holies and only came out once a year. (p.38)

Tasks must be worthwhile to pupils, and the word 'worthwhile' carries a
double edge. The tasks must be seen to be worthwhile by pupils, and they
must make a worthwhile contribution to their religious education!

Activities and subject matter

In conclusion we may reflect on the relation of activities and subject matter.
I have often found it useful to think about how children learn within a religious
tradition. The festivals of Judaism offer a marvellous resource and suggest
numerous learning experiences and activities for the classroom. Again, listing
the resources a book on the Eucharist, on worship, on community or on any
other aspect of Christian tradition, utilises may suggest certain activities. Thus
work on a parish in Alan Brown's book, *Christian Communities* (Cambridge,
Lutterworth Press, 1982), takes up parish magazines.

A parish magazine will give you a list of people who have duties in the parish.
It will list other things like clubs and societies. In a small group, collect different
magazines and note down the similarities and differences.

Doing this offers an insight into community life. Note too that the task is 'open':
the teacher must co-ordinate the discoveries children make. Sometimes tasks,
although related to content, are too open. The direction, 'Find out more about',
may be daunting for the child and too much for a tired teacher to take on
board − even though it extends the subject matter and preserves his or her
autonomy!

Finally, activities may also be assessed by how far they build bridges between
the pupil and the content, especially where the content may seem difficult
to put across. For example, how do you begin to convey Christians' feelings
for the Bible to pupils? Well, one way which has not been unpopular, I'm
told, is on p.4 of Peter Curtis' book, *The Christians' Book* (Cambridge,
Lutterworth Press, 1984). So 'Find out more'! But reflect too on the role you
will need to play to achieve the author's aims!

Good resources make learning more interesting and engaging − but they
don't make the teacher redundant!

NOTES

1. Rankin, J. (1982) *Christian Worship,* Cambridge, Lutterworth Press
Erricker, C. (1984) *Christian Ethics*, Cambridge, Lutterworth Press
Throughout this chapter extracts taken from recently published textbooks on the Christian tradition *illustrate* different ways in which books may contribute to the process of learning; they are not intended to be evaluative of a whole book.

2. I refer here to:
John Bailey, *Religion in life* (*1. Religious Buildings and Festivals*, 1984, and *2. Founders, Prophets and Sacred Books*, 1985) Huddersfield, Schofield, Sims Ltd

Olivia Bennett, *Exploring Religion* Series (People Buildings Worship Writings Festivals Signs and Symbols) London, Bell & Hyman Ltd, 1985
Both series include Christianity among other world faiths!

Richard Hughes, *A Secondary Religious Education Course,* Oxford University Press
  Book 1 *Christianity Then and Now* 1982
  Book 2 *The Kingdom of Heaven* 1982
  Book 3 *Belief* 1983

3. See, for example, Richard Hughes (1982), *The Kingdom of Heaven* pp.68ff, pp.8ff.

4. Gray, I.A.S. and McFarlen, D.M. (1984) *Search: The Christian Experience*, Glasgow, Blackie.

5. Teachers interested in poster material will find many ideas for using posters in Taylor, N. and Bloodworth, J. (1980) *Living with Posters,* London, Ikon Productions and USPG).

6. See Thorley, S. (1984) *Christianity in Words and Pictures,* Exeter, RMEP.

7. Hines, B. (1968) *Kes,* Harmondsworth, Penguin Books

8. Hughes, R. (1983) *Christianity Then and Now,* Oxford University Press (section entitled 'A note to the teacher')

22   A Bibliography for the teaching of Christianity

Peter Doble & Mary Hayward

The passage of time since the publication of *Teaching Christianity* in 1987 has led us to make substantial changes to both the format and the content of the bibliographies which follow. Books which have been retained from the first printing are indicated by an asterisk; we believe that they still contain useful information, but some will need to be read mindful of their date of publication; this is true particularly of those books which offer a worldwide perspective, especially where it pertains to Eastern Europe.

BOOKS FOR TEACHERS

Bibliographies for Christianity are immense and any short selection inevitably reflects some degree of personal preference, although our concern has been for breadth and for depth in relation to the themes covered in the earlier sections of this book. Impartial and objective studies of Christianity as a world religion remain few and readers will find that many of the books listed are written from within the tradition; additionally, the books listed will, of course, direct the reader to further subject specific bibliographies.

Surveys

Banks, R. et al., *The Quiet Revolution*, Lion 1985/1989
Barrett, D.B., *World Christian Encyclopaedia*, OUP 1982*
McKenzie, P., *The Christians*, SPCK 1988
Smart, N., *The Phenomenon of Christianity*, Collins 1979*

The Christian Church: global and historical perspectives

Allan, J.D., *The Evangelicals*, Paternoster 1989
Board, D.M. (ed.), *A Way of Life: Being a Catholic Today*, Collins 1982*
Boff, L. & C., *Introducing Liberation Theology*, Burns & Oates 1987
Broun, J., *Conscience and Captivity*, Ethics and Public Policy Centre 1988
Chadwick, H. & Evans, G.R., *Atlas of the Christian Church*, Macmillan 1987
Hastings, A., *A History of English Christianity 1920-1990*, SCM 1990
Moorman, J.R.H., *The Anglican Spiritual Tradition*, DLT 1983*
Parratt, J. (ed.), *A Reader in African Christian Theology*, SPCK 1987
Pirouet, L., *Christianity Worldwide*, SPCK 1989
Sugirtharajah R.S. & Hargreaves C., *Readings in Indian Christian Theology 1*, SPCK 1993
Ware, T., *The Orthodox Way*, Mowbray 1979*

Jesus/New Testament

Court, J. & K., *The New Testament World*, CUP 1990
Houlden, J.L., *Jesus: A Question of Identity*, SPCK 1992
Theissen, G., *The Shadow of the Galilean*, SCM 1987
Tuckett, C.M., *Reading the New Testament*, SPCK 1987
Vermes, G., *Jesus and the World of Judaism*, SCM 1983*

Worship

Clowney P. & T., *Exploring Churches*, Lion 1993 edn.
Davies J.G., *A New Dictionary of Liturgy and Worship*, SCM 1986*
Metford, J.C.J., *The Christian Year*, Thames & Hudson 1991
Wainwright, G., *Doxology*, Epworth 1980

Visual Expression

Moore, P., *Christianity*, Ward Lock 1982*
Scharper, P. & S., *The Gospel in Art by the Peasants of Solentiname*, Orbis Books 1984
Takenaka, M. & O'Grady, R., *The Bible through Asian Eyes*, Pace Publishing/Asian Christian Art 1991. (Available in UK through CCBI, 35 Lower Marsh Street, London SE1 7RL).
Wessels, A., *Images of Jesus*, SCM 1990

Values and Issues

Cragg, K., *The Christ and the Faiths*, SPCK 1986
Forrester, D.B., *Theology and Politics*, Blackwell 1988

Gill, R., *Christian Ethics in Secular Worlds*, T & T Clark 1991
Gill, R., *A Textbook of Christian Ethics*, T & T Clark 1985
Jones, R.G., *Groundwork of Christian Ethics*, Epworth 1984
Macquarrie, J., *A Dictionary of Christian Ethics*, SCM 1984*

BOOKS FOR THE CLASSROOM

This section consists mainly of material published since the first printing of this book. Since most of the books listed take a broad approach to Christianity, we have not attempted to classify these according to subjects covered; they are simply listed in alphabetical order, usually of author, with an indication of their appropriateness to key stages and for teachers. The focus is on Christianity rather than textual studies of the Gospels; the many books for GCSE groups relating to such studies are not therefore included here.

Brown A.S., *The Christian World*, Macdonald 1984, Simon & Schuster 1992 (pbk) *KS2/3* *
Brown A.S. & Perkins, J., *Christianity*, Batsford 1988 *KS4/GCSE reference*

*The Chichester Project,** Lutterworth/Clarke: *KS3/4*
1 Rankin, J., *Christian Worship*, 1982
2 Brown, A., *Christian Communities*, 1982
3 Erricker, C., *Christian Experience*, 1982
4 Shannon, T., *Jesus*, 1982
5 Curtis, P., *Exploring the Bible*, 1984
6 Curtis, P., *The Christians' Book*, 1984
7 Shannon, T., *Christmas and Easter*, 1984
8 Erricker, C., *Christian Ethics*, 1984
9 Rankin, J., *The Eucharist*, 1985
   Curtis, P., *Christianity*, 1986 *KS2/3*

Cole, W.O., *Christianity*, Stanley Thornes, 1989 *KS4/GCSE*
Cole, W.O., *Discovering Sacred Texts: The Christian Bible*, Heinemann Educational 1993 *KS3*
Cole, W. O. & Mantin, R., *Teaching Christianity*, Heinemann Educational 1994
Courtie, B. & Johnson, M., *Christianity Explored*, Lion 1990 *KS4/GCSE*
Cush, D., *et al.*, *Christians in Britain Today*, Hodder & Stoughton 1991 *KS3/4*
Hammond, J. & Jacob, M., *Christian Belief & Practice*, Oliver & Boyd, 1990 *KS4*
Holm, J. & Ridley, R., *Growing up in Christianity*, Longman 1990 *KS3*
Hughes, R.O., *Christianity*, Longman 1991 *KS4/GCSE*
Hughes, R.O., *Religion through Festivals: Christianity*, Longman 1989 *KS3*
Jenkins, J., *Examining Religions: Christianity*, Heinemann Educational 1995 *KS4/GCSE*
Jenkins, J., *Examining Religions: Contemporary Moral Issues*, Heinemann Educational, 1992 ed. *KS4/GCSE*
Jenkins, J., *Introducing Moral Issues*, Heinemann Educational 1994 *KS3*
Jenkins, S. & Smith, L., *Christianity in Today's World*, BBC 1992 *KS4/GCSE*
Lealman, B., *Christian Buildings*, CEM 1990 *KS3/4T*

Living Festivals Series: RMEP *KS3/4*
Ewens, A., *Advent*, 1987
Sampson, F., *Ascensiontide and Pentecost*, 1986

Earlier titles include *Christmas, Shrove Tuesday, Ash Wednesday and Lent, Holy Week*, and *Easter.**

Mayled, J., *Christian Festivals*, 1988 (Teacher book of photocopiable masters).

Minney, R., *Christianity for GCSE*, Blackwell 1989 (now available from Simon & Schuster) **KS4/GCSE**

Morton, S.A., *Encounters: a sketchbook of world Christianity*, CEM 1992 **KS4/T**

Read, G., Rudge J. & Howarth, R.B., **The Westhill Project: RE 5-16** Stanley Thornes (formerly Mary Glasgow)
Christianity: Teacher's Manual 1986
Christians 3 1987 **KS3**
Christians 4 1987 **KS4**

Richards, C. & H., *Christianity: A Way of Life*, Blackie 1991 **KS4/GCSE**
What the Churches say on Moral and Social Issues, CEM 1991 **KS4/T**

Windsor, G. & Hughes, J., **Exploring Christianity Series:** Heinemann Educational 1990
Jesus and the Birth of the Church
Worship and Festivals
The Bible and Christian Belief
Christian Life, Personal and Social Issues **KS3**

Wintersgill, B., *Christianity: a Living Faith*, Macmillan 1989 **KS4/GCSE**
Wood, A., *Being a Christian*, BFSS National RE Centre 1990 **KS3**

AUDIO - VISUAL RESOURCES

There has not been any substantial increase in the range of AVA resources on Christianity which are appropriate for school. Many of the materials available in 1987 remain so or are likely to be available from RE Centres; modifications to our earlier list are not substantial, and here it is the *new materials* which are indicated by an asterisk.

Slides

There is an excellent series of slides, *People at Worship*, relating to Christian festivals, worship, symbols and buildings. Published by *The Slide Centre*, their quality is very good, and the selection of topics is helpful to the presentation of Christian practice. Among them are:

S1411 *Christian Worship: Anglican Communion* (18 slides).
S1416 *Christian Worship: Baptist* (18 slides).
S1462 *Christian Initiation: Infant Baptism and Confirmation* (21 slides).
S1463 *Christian Initiation: Dedication and Believers' Baptism* (15 slides).
S1464 *Christian Churches: the Significant Features* (24 slides).
S1465 *Christian Symbols* (24 slides).
S1466 *A Christian Wedding* (12 slides).
S1473 *Holy Week: Palm Sunday and Maundy Thursday* (18 slides).
S1474 *Holy Week: Good Friday* (12 Slides).

S1475 *Holy Week: Holy Saturday and Easter Day* (18 slides).

Bury Peerless has produced seventy slides on *Christianity in India* concerning its historical development from the arrival of St Thomas the Apostle to the present day.

CEM have produced a sequence of 24 slides and tape by Brenda Lealman on *Christ in Art*.

Posters

The *Pictorial Charts Educational Trust* have published a series of posters which, although designed to cover a number of religious traditions, offer visual material for the teaching of Christianity. Their titles are self-explanatory:

E720 *Birth Rites*
E721 *Initiation Rites*
E722 *Marriage Rites*
E723 *Death Rites*
E724 *Holy Places*
E728 *Places of Worship*
E729 *Days of Worship*
although the selection and presentation of material will not be to everyone's taste. Two of the posters in their
E725 *Holy Writings*
offer material on the Greek and Latin Bible, and
E726 *Holy Books*
features Christianity, the Bible being among the collection.
E745 *Christian Festivals*
comprises four charts concerning Christmas, Easter, Whitsun and Harvest.

Similarly poster sets E732, E733, E734 on *Religion in Art** contain some posters drawn from the Christian tradition, as does *My Religion.** Wallchart *Christianity in Today's World** provides an overview.

The Westhill Project: RE 5-16 have produced a photopack of 20 pictures with detailed notes which accompany their books (see above) but may also be used independently.*

Video

This remains a disappointing area. While much might be achieved through this most popular of all media, only a few productions offer much for the study of Christianity.

The well known series from Central Independent Television *Believe it or not* is available in full on four videos;* the series as a whole includes many programmes on Christianity, whilst a new series *What's it Like . . . ?* (1994)*

also includes Christianity. Central Television's Religion catalogue, containing many programmes on religious topics for the general viewer which also have potential for school, is obtainable from their Video Resource Unit, Broad Street, Birmingham B1 2JP.

Precision Video has produced a four-cassette version of Franco Zeffirelli's *Jesus of Nazareth* which has the virtue of stressing Jesus' Jewishness.

CTVC have produced *Jesus Christ Movie Star* which explores interpretations of the Jesus story in the cinema.*

CEM Video has produced a series on different faiths: *Through the Eyes of . . . Children* (Sikh, Hindu, Jewish, Muslim, *et al.*) but *Christianity Through the Eyes of Christian Children* is sufficiently different from the others in style and approach to elicit a large measure of disappointment. Their *Quakerism through the eyes of . . .* is a rather more successful production, though it will be visually 'dated' in parts.

The Exmouth School Department of Religion has explored its own way of providing resources. Video films of places or events significant for, or distinctive of, faith communities are offered without commentary but with notes, allowing a great flexibility in classroom use. In this *Videotext series, World Religions: Aspects of Christianity* offers footage of a Catholic Mass, Salvation Army Meeting, Parish Church, Orthodox Easter Night Procession, Baptism in a Baptist Church, and an Anglican Wedding.

These two series are available from Chansitor Publications Ltd., St. Mary's Works, Norwich NR3 3BH

Christianity in Today's World (BBC)* is more recent and explores Christianity's engagement with a number of contemporary issues in a variety of cultural contexts.

Christian Art (Arlosh Educational Resources, Farmington Institute)* explores the work of 3 contemporary artists and might be of interest from Key Stage KS3 onwards.

Acknowledgement

The compilers are grateful to Heinemann Education for permission to draw on bibliographies recently prepared for **Teaching World Religions** (1993) in revising this chapter.

Appendix: The aims of the Chichester Project

The Chichester Project is concerned with the production of material for teaching Christianity in secondary schools. It is a research project supported by many professionals in the field of Religious Education. It tries to foster an open approach to the teaching of Christianity in accordance with the following principles.

Principles

1. Although Christianity is to be seen as a world religion, it will probably provide the material for the greater part of most RE syllabuses, as it fugures largely in the cultural life of Britain, and in the moral foundation of her government.
2. Acceptance or rejection of Christian tenets is not the direct concern of the teacher. The material should be capable of being used without offence to pupils of any faith. The aim of Religious Education is 'understanding'. It is of the utmost importance to this country that pupils come to *understand* Christianity in its many forms. This is educationally important in itself, but it also contributes to a more general capacity for religious understanding.
3. The project begins with the assumption that religious sensibility is an essential dimension of human development, and that however diverse its manifestations it is an inherent human capacity. We believe that the awakening and educating of this sensibility, which is fundamental to the understanding of religion, is the prime task of the RE teacher.

Method

The first material produced for the project was in the form of pupils' books. Each book is prepared by an individual. Every attempt has been made to give individual authors the benefit of professional insights and opinions,

but no attempt has been made to obtain a uniformity of treatment. RE teachi
should have the benefit of *variety* as much as any other good teaching.

Each book bears the style of the individual author. Note further, that eac
book is a separate entity. We have not attempted to produce a course. It
hoped that the material can be fitted into syllabuses devised by teachers an
schools.

In general, the approach is to begin with an aspect of Christian practi
or experience which can be observed, and to proceed to ask questions abo
it. Too often in the past, Christianity has been approached solely from a stud
of the New Testament — indeed, usually only the Gospels — and sometim
only one Gospel! We wish to encourage the study of the New Testament, b
this alone will not be enough to equip students to understand fully th
expressions of Christianity which they will encounter.

Pupils will, it is hoped, discover that religious beliefs and practices ar
intrinsically interesting and that some might even have meaning for their ow
lives.

The role of the teacher

From what has been said about the general principles, some might conclud
that the teacher who possesses Christian convictions has to suppress them
This is not the case. Indeed, the teacher's convictions can often become
valuable resource for pupils trying to discover some of the things that it mean
to be a Christian. This should not, however, contradict the principle whic
leaves pupils free, and it should hardly be necessary to caution teachers again
pressing for any kind of religious allegiance on the part of pupils. Any suc
attempt would contradict the nature of the materials.

It cannot be emphasised too strongly, however, that material is only materi
and we confidently expect teachers to enliven and enrich these outlines fro
their own experiences and resources. Nor is it expected that classes shoul
slavishly follow all the suggested exercises and activities. These should b
apportioned according to the teacher's more intimate knowledge of a clas
and of individual pupils.

Each book has a bibliography which could be useful in pursuing the top
further.

The Chichester Project is an ongoing research project supported by the Sha
Working Party for World Religion in Education and the West Sussex Institu
for Higher Education. Grants have been made by the Spalding Trusts, A
Saints' Trust, and the United Society for Christian Literature. Further source
of finance are being sought. The project is a registered charity. Teachers ar
invited to send their comments and suggestions on the material, to assist furthe
development.

John Rankin
Project Director